The Acquirer's Multiple: How the Billionaire Contrarians of Deep Value Beat the Market

TOBIAS E. CARLISLE

DEDICATION

For Nick, Stell, Tom, and Olly.

CONTENTS

PREFACE

"It is better to be lucky. But I would rather be exact.
Then when luck comes, you are ready."
—Ernest Hemingway, *The Old Man and The Sea* (1952)

This book is a short, simple explanation of one of the most powerful ideas in investing: zig.

Zig?

Zig when the crowd zags. Zig with the value investors. Zig with the contrarians.

Here's why: the only way to get a good price is to buy what the crowd wants to sell and sell what the crowd wants to buy. It means a low price. And it might mean the stock is undervalued. That's a good thing. It means the downside is smaller than the upside. If we're wrong, we won't lose much. If we're right, we could make a lot.

When we find undervalued stocks, we often find they are cheap for a reason: the business looks bad. Why buy an undervalued stock with a seemingly bad business? Because the markets are ruled by a powerful force known as *mean reversion*: the idea that things go back toward normal.

Mean reversion pushes up undervalued stocks. And it pulls down expensive stocks. It pulls down fast-growing, profitable businesses, and it pushes up shrinking loss-makers. It works on stock markets, industries, and whole economies. It is the business cycle: the boom after the bust and the bust after the boom.

The best investors know this. They expect the turn in a stock's fortunes. While the crowd imagines the trend continues forever, deep-value investors and contrarians zig before it turns.

Mean reversion has two important consequences for investors:

1. Undervalued, out-of-favor stocks tend to beat the market. Glamorous, expensive stocks don't.

2. Fast-growing businesses tend to slow down. Highly profitable businesses tend to become less profitable. The reverse is also true. Flatlining or declining businesses tend to turn around and start growing again. Unprofitable businesses tend to become more profitable.

This might be a surprise if you're familiar with the way billionaire Warren Buffett invests. He is a value investor who buys undervalued stocks. But he only buys a special group with sustainable high profits. He calls them "wonderful companies at fair prices." And he prefers them to "fair companies at wonderful prices": those that are undervalued but with mixed profitability.

Billion-dollar fund manager Joel Greenblatt tested Buffett's wonderful companies at fair prices idea. He found it beat the market, and he wrote about it in a great 2006 book called *The Little Book That Beats the Market*. It is one of the most successful books on investing ever written.

We ran our own test on Greenblatt's book and found that he was right. Buffett's wonderful companies at fair prices do beat the market. But here's the twist: fair companies at wonderful prices do even better.

In this book, I show how to find those fair companies at wonderful prices. And I explain in plain and simple terms why they beat Buffett's wonderful companies at fair prices.

We wrote about the test in 2012 and again in my 2014 book, *Deep Value*. It did well for an expensive, quasi-academic textbook on valuation and corporate governance. But I wanted one that could be read by non-professional investors.

This book is intended to be a pocket field-guide to fair companies at wonderful prices. Its mission is to help spread the contrarian message. It's a collection of the best ideas from my books *Deep Value*, *Quantitative Value*, and *Concentrated Investing*. In this book, the ideas in those are simplified, summarized, and expanded.

The book is based on talks I have given at Harvard, Cal Tech, Google, the New York Society of Security Analysts (NYSSA), the Chartered Financial Analysts Association of Los Angeles (CFA LA), and others.

My work has been featured in *Forbes*, *The Harvard Business Review*, *The Journal of Applied Corporate Finance*, two editions of the Booth Cleary *Introduction to Corporate Finance*, and the *Manual of Ideas*. I've talked about the ideas in it on Bloomberg TV and radio, Yahoo Finance, Sky Business, and NPR, among others.

The overwhelming response is disbelief. The reason? Many find the ideas counterintuitive—in conflict with our intuition about the way the world works. A few, however, find the ideas wholly intuitive.

You don't need to be a lawyer, a chartered financial analyst, a tech genius, or a Harvard graduate to get this book. Buffett wrote in 1984, "It is extraordinary to me that the idea of buying dollar bills for 40 cents takes immediately to people or it doesn't take at all":[1]

A fellow…who had no formal education in business, understands immediately the value approach to investing and he's applying it five minutes later.

In the book, I set out the data and my reasoning. We'll look at the details of actual stock picks by billionaire deep-value investors:

- Warren Buffett
- Carl Icahn
- Daniel Loeb, and
- David Einhorn

We'll see the strategies of Buffett and his teacher, Benjamin Graham, and other contrarians, including:

- billionaire *trader* Paul Tudor Jones
- *venture capitalist* billionaire Peter Thiel, and
- *global macroinvestor* billionaire Michael Steinhardt

I wrote this book so you can read it in a couple of hours. It's written for my kids, family, and friends, for people who are smart but not *stock-market people*. That means it's written in plain English. Where I need to define a stock-market term, I've tried to do it as simply as possible. And this book is packed with charts and drawings explaining why it's important to zig when the crowd zags. You'll learn why fair stocks at wonderful prices beat the market *and* wonderful stocks at fair prices. Let's get started.

TOBIAS E. CARLISLE

ACKNOWLEDGMENTS

I am grateful to the early reviewers of this book, notably
Johnny Hopkins, Jacob Taylor and Lonnie Rush at Farnam
Street Investments, Michael Seckler and John Alberg at
Euclidean Technologies, and my wife, Nick.

ABOUT THE AUTHOR

Tobias Carlisle is the founder and managing director of Acquirers Funds, LLC. He serves as portfolio manager of Acquirers Funds managed accounts and funds.

He is the author of the bestselling book *Deep Value: Why Activists Investors and Other Contrarians Battle for Control of Losing Corporations* (2014, Wiley Finance). He is a coauthor of *Concentrated Investing: Strategies of the World's Greatest Concentrated Value Investors* (2016, Wiley Finance) and *Quantitative Value: A Practitioner's Guide to Automating Intelligent Investment and Eliminating Behavioral Errors* (2012, Wiley Finance). His books have been translated into five languages. Tobias also runs the websites AcquirersMultiple.com—home of The Acquirer's Multiple stock screeners—and Greenbackd.com. His Twitter handle is @greenbackd.

He has broad experience in investment management, business valuation, corporate governance, and corporate law. Before founding the precursor to Acquirers Funds in 2010, Tobias was an analyst at an activist hedge fund, general counsel of a company listed on the Australian Stock Exchange, and a corporate advisory lawyer. As a lawyer specializing in mergers and acquisitions, he has advised on deals across a range of industries in the United States, the United Kingdom, China, Australia, Singapore, Bermuda, Papua New Guinea, New Zealand, and Guam.

He is a graduate of the University of Queensland in Australia with degrees in law (2001) and business (management) (1999).

1. HOW THE BILLIONAIRE CONTRARIANS ZIG

"To beat the market you have to do something different from the market."
—Joel Greenblatt, *Talks at Google*, April 4, 2017.

Zig /zig/ (verb): To make a sharp change in direction. Used in contrast to zag: *When the crowd zags, zig!*

The billionaire contrarians of deep value zig when the crowd zags.

They buy *what* the crowd wants to sell. They sell *when* the crowd wants to buy.

They buy stocks with falling prices.

...with falling profits.

...that lose money.

...that are failing.

...that have failed.

But they only do it when the stock is deeply undervalued.

Billionaire value-investor Warren Buffett famously says he tries to be "fearful when others are greedy, and greedy when others are fearful." Said in other words, Buffett zigs when the crowd zags.

Like Buffett, billionaire corporate-raider Carl Icahn is also a value investor. He has been called "the contrarian to end all contrarians."[2] Ken Moelis, former chief of investment banking at UBS, said of Icahn, "He'll buy at the worst possible moment, when there's no reason to see a sunny side and no one agrees with him."[3] Icahn explains why:[4]

> The consensus thinking is generally wrong. If you go with a trend, the momentum always falls apart on you. So I buy companies that are not glamorous and usually out of favor. It's even better if the whole industry is out of favor.

Icahn zigs when the crowd zags.

Billionaire trader Paul Tudor Jones is a well-known contrarian. In Jack D. Schwager's *Market Wizards* (1989), he said:

> I learned that even though markets look their very best when they are setting new highs, that is often the best time to sell. To some extent, to be a good trader, you have to be a contrarian.

Paul Tudor Jones zigs when the market zags.

Billionaire investor Peter Thiel draws this diagram to describe the "sweet spot" for his chosen stocks:

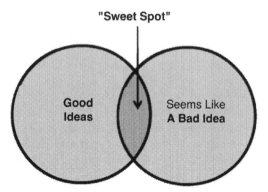

"Sweet Spot"

Good Ideas

Seems Like A Bad Idea

Sweet Spot: A Good Idea That Seems Like a Bad Idea
Source: Paul Graham, "Black Swan Farming," September 2012,
Available at http://www.paulgraham.com/swan.html

Thiel's "sweet spot" is a good idea that seems like a bad idea to the crowd. But Thiel thinks it might be a good idea. Thiel's zigging while the crowd zags.

Billionaire global macroinvestor Michael Steinhardt made his investors about five-hundred times their money over thirty years until 1995. In his autobiography, Steinhardt described how he told an intern what he looked for:[5]

> I told him that ideally he should be able to tell me, in two minutes, four things: (1) the idea; (2) the consensus view; (3) his variant perception; and (4) a trigger event. No mean feat. In those instances where there was no variant perception…I generally had no interest and would discourage investing.

Steinhardt's "variant perception" is a view that is different from the crowd's. Steinhardt tries to zig while the crowd zags.

Billionaire global macroinvestor Ray Dalio says:[6]

You have to be an independent thinker in markets to be successful because the consensus is built into the price. You have to have a view that's different from the consensus.

Dalio is saying you only beat the market if you zig.

Billionaire distressed debt investor Howard Marks says, "To achieve superior investment results, you have to hold nonconsensus views regarding value, and they have to be accurate."[7] Venture capitalist Andy Rachleff says Marks thinks about investments in a two-by-two grid that looks like this:

Outsized Returns: Right and Nonconsensus

Source: Andy Rachleff, "Demystifying Venture Capital Economics, Part 1," Available at https://blog.wealthfront.com/venture-capital-economics/

On one side, you can either be "Consensus"—go with the crowd—or be "Nonconsensus"—*zig*. On the other side, you can be *right* or *wrong*. Rachleff explains his grid:[8]

Now obviously if you're wrong you don't make money. The only way as an investor and as an entrepreneur to make outsized returns is by being right and nonconsensus.

You don't beat the market if you're wrong or if you zag with the crowd.

The last one surprises many new investors. You don't beat the market if you're right and you zag along with the crowd? Nope. You don't beat the market when you're right if the crowd has already decided the stock is a good one. The reason? As we'll see, you pay a high price that reflects the crowd's high hopes for the stock. Even if the stock meets those high hopes, it won't beat the market.

You can't beat the market by zagging along with it. To beat it, you must zig as the crowd zags. Here's why: the only way to get a low price is to buy what the crowd wants to sell and sell when the crowd wants to buy.

A *low* price means a price lower than the stock's value. It means an unfair, lopsided bet: a small downside and a big upside. A small downside means the price already includes the worst-case scenario. That gives us a margin of error. If we're wrong, we won't lose much. If we're right, we'll make a lot. A bigger upside means we break even, though we have more losses than successes. If we manage to succeed as often as or more often than we make mistakes, we'll do well.

But it's not enough to be a mere contrarian. We must also be right. Steinhardt says, "To be contrarian and to be right in your judgement when the consensus is wrong is where you get the golden ring. And it doesn't happen that much. But when it does happen you make extraordinary amounts of money."[9]

Billionaire value-investor Seth Klarman says, "Value investing is at its core the marriage of a contrarian streak and a calculator."[10] Klarman is saying that we should do some work. It's not enough that the crowd doesn't want a stock. We should figure out if we *do*. For that, we look at the company's fundamentals.

What are a company's fundamentals? Buffett's teacher, Benjamin Graham, taught him that a share is an ownership stake in a company. It's not just a ticker symbol. Thinking like an owner implies three ideas:

1. We should know what the company does. What is its business? How does it make money?

2. We should know what it owns. What are its assets? What does it owe?

3. We should know who runs it and who owns it. Is management doing a good job? Are the big shareholders paying attention?

Sometimes investors use *company* (or *corporation*) and *business* as substitutes. They are different. A company is a legal entity. It owns the assets. It employs the staff. It enters into the contracts. It can sue and be sued. Business is the activity of selling goods or services with the aim of making a profit. Shareholders own shares in the company. The company owns the business and the assets.

A business can be worth a lot, worthless, or worth less than nothing if it's regularly losing money. Also, a company can have lots of value, or it can have a negative value if it owes more than the assets it owns. Many investors closely watch profits—the fruits of the business—but ignore assets, including cash.

We often find undervalued stocks are cheap for a reason: the business is bad or poorly managed. Glamorous, fast-growing, or highly profitable businesses command high prices. Undervaluation results from flatlining growth, falling profits, losses, or looming failure. Why buy a company with a failing business, even if it is undervalued?

There are three reasons:

1. It might have valuable assets. The crowd often sells a stock based on its business alone, ignoring its cash and other assets.

2. Many seemingly scary, bad, or boring businesses turn out to be less scary, bad, or boring than they seem.

3. Poorly managed companies attract outside investors who might buy them or turn them around. This is what private equity firms and activists do for a living. But shareholders don't have to wait on other investors. They have rights as owners, and they exercise those rights by voting at meetings. With enough votes, shareholders can change a company's bad policies.

These three reasons create opportunities for contrarians with calculators. This is why we seek out stocks that lose money or seem like bad ideas, and it's why we ignore the crowd. Undervalued and out-of-favor companies offer the chance to zig—to buy something valuable that someone else wants to sell too cheaply.

Companies become undervalued because businesses hit a bump in the road. The crowd overreacts. Or else the business is boring and the crowd grows impatient. When an undervalued company owns a scary, bad, or boring business, often all it needs is time. Given enough time, many businesses turn out to be less scary, boring, or bad as they seem at first. A seemingly poor business with a lot of asset value can be a good bet. If the business improves, it can be a great bet.

How do we know if any given bad business will get better with time? We don't. But we know many bad businesses will. The reason is a powerful market force known as *mean reversion*, a technical name for a simple idea: things go back to normal.

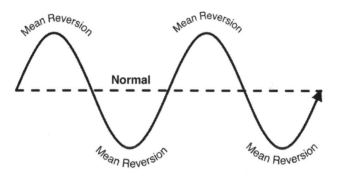

Mean Reversion: Things Go Back Toward Normal

Mean reversion pushes up the prices of undervalued stocks, and it pulls down the prices of expensive stocks.

It returns fast-growing and high-profit businesses to earth, and it points business with falling earnings or growing losses back to the heavens.

It works on stock markets, industries, and whole economies. We know it as the booms and busts of the business cycle or the peaks and troughs of the stock market.

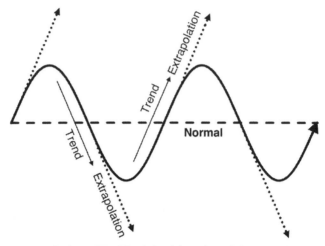

Extrapolation: We Find the Trend and Extrapolate It

Mean reversion is the *expected* outcome. But *we* don't expect mean reversion. Instead, our instinct is to find a trend and extrapolate it. We think it will always be winter for some stocks and summer for others. Instead, fall follows summer, and spring follows winter. Eventually.

This is the secret to contrarian investing: the turns are hidden. If they were as predictable as winter after fall or summer after spring, we'd quickly find the pattern. Instead, it's random.

What causes mean reversion? How does the high-growth, high-profit stock fall back to average? How does the undervalued stock rise to fair value?

Benjamin Graham once described this as "one of the mysteries of our business."[11] He was being a little modest. The microeconomic answer is simple-ish. The answer is *competition.*

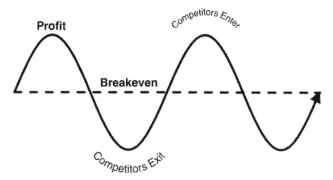

Competition: Growth and Profits Attract Competitors

Fast growth and high profits attract competitors—entrepreneurs and businesses in related industries. Competitors eat away at the growth and profit.

Losses cause competitors to fold or simply leave the industry, and the lack of competition creates a time of high growth and profit for the surviving businesses.

Billionaire value-investor Jeremy Grantham knows profits are mean reverting:[12]

> Profit margins are probably the most mean-reverting series in finance, and if profit margins do not mean-revert, then something has gone badly wrong with capitalism. If high profits do not attract competition, there is something wrong with the system and it is not functioning properly.

Buffett agrees. He wrote in 1999 that you must be wildly optimistic to believe profits can remain high for any sustained period. He said:[13]

> One thing keeping the percentage [of corporate profits] down will be competition, which is alive and

well.

The ebbing and flowing of competitors cause mean reversion at the business level, but what causes it at the company level? How do undervalued and expensive stocks get back to fair value? The answer is other investors. Fundamental investors. Value investors.

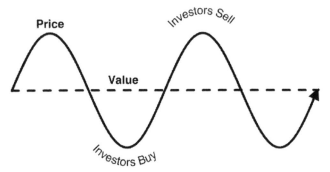

Fundamentals: Undervaluation Attracts Investors

Undervalued assets and profits attract investors. Value investors and other fundamental investors start to buy stock and so push up stock prices.

Expensive assets and profits cause those investors to sell. The selling pushes down stock prices.

Mean reversion has two important implications for investors:

1. Undervalued, out-of-favor stocks tend to beat the market. The more undervalued the stock, the greater the return. Value investors call the difference between the market price and the underlying value the *margin of safety*.

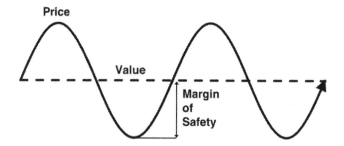

Margin of Safety: The Bigger, the Better the Return

The bigger the margin of safety, the better the return. This is why we ignore advice like the old saying, "Never catch a falling knife." Undervalued stocks are lower risk than glamorous, expensive stocks, which have no margin of safety.

2. Fast-growth or highly profitable businesses tend to slow down or become less profitable. Declining or unprofitable businesses tend to do better.

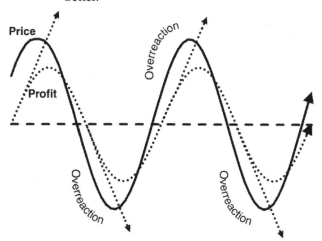

Overreaction: Price Over-/Underestimates Profit

Investors make the error worse by overpaying for unsustainable growth or profit. They extrapolate out the profit trend and buy. If the stock delivers on the promised growth or profit, it only earns a market return. If it doesn't, it gets crushed.

Value investors take the other side of this trade. Where the stock price discounts even the worst-case scenario, the worst-case scenario can lead to market-beating returns. If something better than the worst-case scenario occurs—if profits or growth return—the returns can be tremendous.

Without knowing when it will occur, value investors and other contrarians expect the turn in a stock's fortunes.

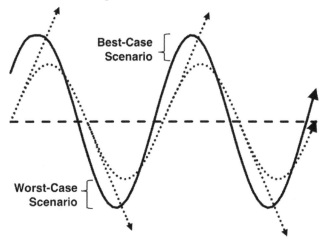

Best-Case
Scenario

Worst-Case
Scenario

The Worst-Case Scenario: Time to Buy

They buy at what looks like the worst possible time, when profits are falling or losses are widening, and it looks like this will continue until the crashing stock hits zero. It's the worst-case scenario. But the stock is undervalued, and it offers a wide margin of safety. It's time to buy.

As Klarman says, "High uncertainty is frequently accompanied by low prices. By the time the uncertainty is resolved, prices are likely to have risen."[14]

They'll also sell at what looks like the best possible time: profits are high and rising quickly, and it looks like this will continue forever. The stock price is soaring. It's the best-case scenario. But the stock is expensive, and it offers no margin of safety. It's time to sell.

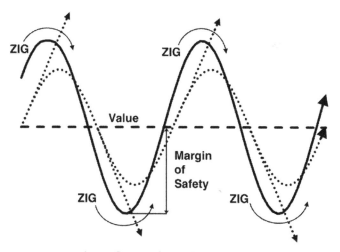

Zig: Contrarians Expect Mean Reversion

While the crowd imagines the profit and stock price trends will continue, value investors and contrarians zig.

The Magic Formula

"You pay a very high price in the stock market
for a cheery consensus."
—Warren Buffett, *Forbes Magazine* (1979)

Buffett buys undervalued stocks. Recall that he only

buys a small, special group with sustained high profits. He calls this group "wonderful companies at fair prices." And he prefers them to "fair companies at wonderful prices": those that are undervalued but with mixed profitability. (We'll explore these concepts in depth in a later chapter.)

Joel Greenblatt tested a simple version of Buffett's wonderful companies at fair prices idea. He found that it beat the market, and he wrote about it in *The Little Book That Beats the Market.* He called Buffett's simple wonderful-companies-at-fair-prices idea the "Magic Formula."

In the book, Greenblatt described how he created his test. We repeated it for this book. (We also talk about our test and the results in detail in chapter 7.) We agree with Greenblatt. The Magic Formula does beat the market, as the next chart shows.

$10,000 Invested in the S&P 500 and the Magic Formula (1973 to 2017)

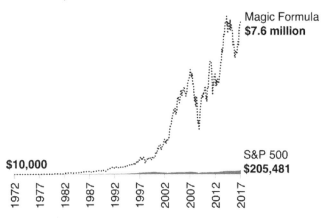

Thirty Stocks with Market Cap $50 Million and Above

The magic formula beats the market, just as Greenblatt

claims. But what's the true cause of the market-beating results?

Here's the twist. Fair companies at wonderful prices— what I call the *Acquirer's Multiple*—do better.

In this test, we buy the most undervalued stocks with no regard for profitability. (We talk about our test and the results in detail in a later chapter.)

$10,000 Invested in the Acquirer's Multiple, Magic Formula, and S&P 500 (1973 to 2017)

Thirty Stocks with Market Cap $50 Million and Above

In our test, the Acquirer's Multiple—fair companies at wonderful prices—beats the Magic Formula—wonderful companies at fair prices. It seems the size of the margin of safety—the market price discount from value—is more important than profitability.

High profits are mean reverting, and falling profits dampen the returns to the Magic Formula. The Acquirer's Multiple buys stocks with mixed profits; some are highly profitable, others break even, and others lose money. It relies on the price mean reverting to the value and the businesses improving.

Does this mean that Buffett is wrong about wonderful companies at fair prices being better than fair companies at wonderful prices? Does Buffett's liking for wonderful companies at fair prices disagree with the idea of mean reversion in profits? In short, no.

Buffett seeks stocks with *sustainable* profits, those that have what he calls a "moat"—in other words, a *competitive advantage*. A moat is something that allows a business to beat its competition.

There are many sources of moats. If a business can make its widget for less, sell it for more, or sell more of it than any other business, it has a moat.

A patent, for example, is a moat. A patent is the sole right to make an invention. If you have one, you can stop everyone else from making your invention for twenty years. If no other business can copy the invention, the owner of the patent has a monopoly and can charge whatever price maximizes its profit.

A well-known brand is also a moat. Coca-Cola can charge more for its cola than store-brand colas. It's not a monopoly, but it allows Coke to earn more profit per can than its competitors.

The problem for investors is it's hard to find businesses that can keep up high profits. We can't predict what businesses will maintain profits. Even if we look for high past profits and the reason why—the moat—most businesses see profits fall over time. In a later chapter, we try to identify moats in a scientific, repeatable way. But our chance of finding a business that can sustain profits is still as good as flipping a coin. There are three reasons why:

1. Only a few businesses have a moat. Most don't. It can be hard to tell a business with a real moat from one that is at the peak of its business cycle.

2. A moat is no guarantee of high profits. Coke's brand allows it to sell its cola for more than other colas. But if tastes change to other sodas, or water, Coke's profits will fall.

3. Moats don't last forever. Newspapers used to have a moat. If you wanted to advertise in a city, you advertised in the local paper. There was no other way. The Internet has changed that relationship. Now, you might advertise with Google or Facebook.

Buffett is a brilliant business analyst—the best alive and perhaps the best who has ever lived. His long memory, gift for numbers, and lifelong devotion to business analysis set him apart. He has a sixth sense for finding moats with relentless profitability. But he didn't start out investing in wonderful companies at fair prices.

Buffett got his start as a value-investing contrarian. He was already rich—he had $34 million in 1972, $200 million in 2017 dollars—when he changed from fair companies to wonderful ones. In the next chapter, we begin with one of his early investments.

2. YOUNG BUFFETT'S HEDGE FUND

"The highest rates of return I've ever achieved were in the 1950s. I killed the Dow. You ought to see the numbers...I think I could make you 50 percent a year on $1 million. No, I know I could. I guarantee that."
—Warren Buffett, *BusinessWeek*, July 5, 1999

The business was on an ugly path. It made huge, detailed paper maps. One map for a small city might weigh as much as 50 pounds. When customers' maps needed upgrades, the business mailed out a sticker to cover the out-of-date part of the map. The company had operated for seventy-five years. Twenty years earlier, it had been a monopoly averaging more than $7 million a year in profit. Now it had to compete with a better technology. Its customer base shrank as customers merged and cut expenses. Profits had fallen more than 80 percent to less than $1 million a year. It had cut dividends five times in eight years. Twenty-seven-year-old Warren Buffett liked what he saw.

The company, Sanborn Map, also owned $60 million in cash and investments worth $65 per share. Yet the shares could be bought for $45. Buffett sent a letter to the investors in his hedge fund. He wrote that the $45 stock price meant either the map business was worth –$20 per share ($45 – $65 = –$20), or the investment portfolio was worth 69 cents on the dollar ($45 ÷ $65 = 0.69) with the map business thrown in for free. Either way, it was undervalued. It was a classic Benjamin Graham value investment.

Benjamin Graham had taught him a simple, powerful idea: buy dollars for 50 cents. Buffett spent his days looking for such stocks. It wasn't easy. Real dollars don't sell for 50 cents. (Fake ones do.) But Graham taught Buffett how to find dollars he could buy for 50 cents.

Graham showed Buffett that sometimes a company owns a dollar, and he could buy it for 50 cents by buying the shares. That's a good deal, but Buffett won't control the dollar. The company will. He will need to make sure the company looks after his dollar.

In the case of Sanborn Map, Buffett found a dollar trading for 69 cents. But how to protect the dollar? Buffett's hedge fund bought every share he could find. In short order, he'd picked up 46,000 shares out of the 105,000 on issue. With 43.8 percent of the company's shares (46,000 ÷ 105,000 = 43.8 percent), Buffett could control the company. He asked the board to pay out the $65 per share to the shareholders. The board refused.

Buffett acted quickly. He used his hedge fund's shareholding to get himself elected to the board. At his first board meeting, he found out why the stock was so cheap. The other board members worked for Sanborn Map's biggest customers. They owned almost no stock and just wanted the maps sold cheaply. Buffett again suggested the company sell the investments and pay the money to the shareholders. The other directors rejected the idea.

At the next meeting, Buffett asked them to use the investments to buy out any stockholder who wanted out. The board agreed, if only to avoid a proxy fight with Buffett. (With 43.8 percent of the stock, Buffett was sure to win.) Half of the 1,600 shareholders who together owned 72 percent of the stock accepted the offer. Instead of cash, shareholders who accepted got $65 worth of investments for their $45 shares, a 44.4 percent return on their investment ($65 ÷ $45 = 44.4 percent).

Sanborn Maps was a typically profitable investment for Buffett. It was also a good example of Buffett's instinct to zig when the crowd zags. The market saw the failing map business. Profits had fallen steadily for more than twenty years. But Buffett looked past the 80 percent drop in profit to the asset value—its $65 per share in cash and investments.

The Buffett Hedge Fund Strategy

"My cigar-butt strategy worked very well while I was managing small sums. Indeed, the many dozens of free puffs I obtained in the 1950s made the decade by far the best of my life for both relative and absolute performance."
—Warren Buffett, "Chairman's Letter" *(1989)*

Buffett has said many times that his best returns came in the 1950s. In 1957, he started a hedge fund called the Buffett Partnership. How did he invest in this early part of his career? He looked for undervalued stocks that met Graham's dollars-for-50-cents rule.

Graham had another name for these 50-cent dollars. He called them *cigar butts*. A "cigar butt found on the street that has only one puff left in it may not offer much of a smoke, but the 'bargain purchase' will make that puff all profit," he said.[15] Sanborn Maps had been a classic example of a cigar butt in 1958. In 1959, he found another one, Dempster Mill Manufacturing Company.

Buffett started buying Dempster at about the same time he was fighting for control of Sanborn. Dempster was a maker of windmills, pumps, tanks, and other farming and fertilizing equipment. It had run into trouble. The business was barely profitable. It made its windmills faster than it could sell them and its inventory had grown too big compared to its small business.

Investors looked at Dempster's low profits and sold it down to half the value of its working capital, which included its bloated inventory. Buffett estimated its net working capital—cash, accounts receivable, and inventory minus all liabilities—at around $35 per share. He guessed the tangible book value—the amount of physical assets owned by the company free of any liabilities—to be much higher, between $50 and $75 per share. He could buy the stock for $16 per share. The business would never be very profitable. But it could be a profitable investment if he could pare down its bloated inventory.

Buffett had started buying stock in 1956, paying as little as $16 per share. He continued to buy stock over the next five years, buying small blocks of shares at an average price of $28. In his 1962 hedge fund letter, Buffett said the stock was undervalued because of a "poor management situation, along with a fairly tough industry situation."[16] Management continued to ignore the inventory problem. Dempster's bankers started getting nervous. The bank threatened to pull its loan and shut down the company. Buffett had to act fast.

Like he had in Sanborn, Buffett used his controlling shareholding to get a board seat. Once in control, he sold down the inventory and other assets of the company. The assets he sold were turned into cash and invested in stocks.

Buffett was almost done when he attracted some unwanted attention. Before he could finish the job, the townsfolk in Beatrice, Nebraska, got upset when he tried to sell the town's only factory. The local paper started a front-page campaign to save it. Under pressure, Buffett sold the factory back to the founder's grandson. The local paper rang the fire siren to celebrate the sale.

The townsfolk might have won the battle, but Buffett won the war. His hedge fund made $20 million, triple its original investment. It was another profitable example of the returns to zigging while the crowd zagged.

In the same letter that he revealed his holding in Dempster, Buffett described his investment strategy. He said he split his investments into three groups:

1. Generals
2. Workouts
3. Control situations

Generals were simply undervalued stocks. Buffett bought the stock at a big discount to its value and sold when the market pushed the price up to the value.

The *workouts* were stocks on a timetable. They did not wait on market action. Some other force put these stocks on a rocket sled. That force was a *corporate action*, a board-level decision that delivered a big return of capital or stock buyback, a liquidation, or a sale of the business.

If a general—one of Buffett's undervalued stocks—stayed undervalued for too long, it might become a *control situation*. Buffett would simply keep buying until he owned enough to control the company. Dempster started out as just another undervalued stock. When the price didn't move, Buffett did.

Over five years, he bought enough to get control of the company. Once on the board, he took several steps to improve the company's value. Those corporate actions helped improve the value of Dempster from between $50 to $72 per share to $80 per share. Buffett's return was even better because he paid only $28 per share on average.

If a general moved up before he got control, he sold out. If it didn't move, or fell, he bought more. The ability to get control of the company was important to Buffett because it gave him control of the stock's destiny. Stocks either moved up or Buffett moved in and fixed them up. It worked. And it worked best in down or sideways markets. Either way, Buffett beat the market like a rented mule.

Coattail Riding

Buffett was happy to invest behind other investors seeking control. He called this "coattail riding" in his 1961 letter. He did this with many of his generals:[17]

> Many times generals represent a form of "coattail riding" where we feel the dominating stockholder group has plans for the conversion of unprofitable or under-utilized assets to a better use. We have done that ourselves in Sanborn and Dempster, but everything else equal we would rather let others do the work. Obviously, not only do the values have to be ample in a case like this, but we also have to be careful whose coat we are holding.

The generals were stocks not needing as much attention

as Buffett's control situations. A dominant stockholder had control, and he or she was busy doing the things Buffett would do if he was in control—selling unprofitable or underused assets and buying back stock. Buffett made sure the stock was undervalued enough and then let the big stockholders do the work. He was also happy to sell out at what he regarded as "fair value to a private owner."[18]

Buffett was always on the lookout for undervalued stocks with a quiet shareholder about to become active. These stocks were at a tipping point. When the big shareholder started doing the things Buffett liked, Buffett knew the stock price would shortly take off.

As long as the stock was undervalued when Buffett bought it, he could wait patiently. But he wouldn't wait forever for the sleeping shareholder to wake up. If the undervalued stock's price did nothing for a long time, Buffett would slowly buy a big shareholding. Then he would take control.

Buffett preferred to let others do the work, but he would take control if the company kept losing money. He knew the ability to take control put him into a win-win position. If the stock went up, he made money. If it went down, he bought more, fixed it up, and made money:[19]

> Our willingness and financial ability to assume a controlling position gives us a two-way stretch on many purchases on our group of generals. If the market changes its opinion for the better, the security will advance in price. If it doesn't, we will continue to acquire stock until we can look to the business itself rather than the market for vindication of our judgment.

Buffett used this win-win method in his hedge fund to

great effect. For the twelve years he ran the fund, he returned 31 percent a year. The chart and table below show his hedge fund's returns.

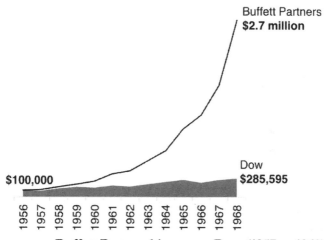

Buffett Partnership versus Dow (1957 to 1968)

Buffett Partnership Performance (1957 to 1968)

Year	Buffett Partnership	Dow Jones
1957	10.4%	−8.4%
1958	40.9%	38.5%
1959	25.9%	20.0%
1960	22.8%	−6.2%
1961	45.9%	22.4%
1962	13.9%	−7.6%
1963	38.7%	20.6%
1964	27.8%	18.7%
1965	47.2%	14.2%
1966	20.4%	−15.6%
1967	35.9%	19.0%
1968	58.8%	7.7%
Average	**31.6%**	**9.1%**

Return

Through his share of the hedge fund and his fees, Buffett turned $100,000 when he was twenty-six years old into a personal stake worth $25 million by the time he was thirty-eight.

Buffett wound up his hedge fund in 1969. He couldn't find enough undervalued stocks to buy. The fund had simply grown too big. Through the fund, he controlled more than $100 million in assets. He said he needed to invest at least $3 million in any stock for it to make a difference. That meant the stock needed a market capitalization, or *market cap*, of at least $100 million. And it had to be a bargain.

In 1969, the market was booming. There simply weren't enough big, undervalued stocks around. If they were undervalued enough, they weren't big enough. If they were big, they weren't undervalued. He told his investors he would wind up the fund. They'd each get cash and shares in the fund's biggest holdings. One would be an undervalued general he found in 1962. That general grew to become a control situation, which he controls to this day.

3. THE GREAT BERKSHIRE HATHAWAY RAID

"In the early days both Warren and I would sometimes
buy control of a company in the market. We don't do that
anymore by the way. We haven't done that for decades but
in the early days we did some of that. Warren bought
control of Berkshire Hathaway in the market."
—Charlie Munger, Interview, *Concentrated Investing* (2016)

Dan Cowin called his thirty-two-year-old buddy Warren
Buffett to give him a stock pick. Cowin was another value
investor. He told Buffett he had found a textile maker called
Berkshire Hathaway in New Bedford, Massachusetts.
Berkshire traded at one-third of its *liquidation value*—the
amount of money they could get out of the company if they
stopped the business and sold the assets for scrap.

Cowin guessed the liquidation value at $22 million, or
$19.46 per share. Berkshire shares traded for $7.50. Buffett
said he knew about Berkshire and agreed it was too
undervalued. But how would he unlock the value?

Cowin said Buffett could easily sell his stock back to the

company. Every two years or so, its president, Seabury Stanton, used the company's cash to buy back its stock. Buffett could buy before Stanton's next buyback and sell to the company then.

If Stanton took too long, Buffett could also take the company over and liquidate it by selling the assets. Cowin knew that he had recently done just that with Sanborn and Dempster. Why not Berkshire? Buffett started buying stock in the company on December 12, 1962. He paid $7.50 for the first two thousand shares and told his broker to keep buying.

By 1963, Buffett's hedge fund was the biggest shareholder in Berkshire. But Buffett wanted his identity kept secret. He asked Cowin to take a seat on Berkshire's board and start sniffing around the company. Cowin quickly found out that Seabury Stanton, the president, fought with the other directors.

One director, Seabury's brother, Otis Stanton, was upset Seabury had picked his own son, Jack, to become the next president of the company. Otis didn't think Jack was up to the job, and he didn't want Jack running the business. Otis preferred another worker, Ken Chace, who ran the factory.

Seabury was also fighting with the company's chairman, who had run the company for almost thirty years. Seabury saw himself as a hero who had saved the company years earlier. He had invested millions of dollars in it when others had been too afraid to keep the business going. He thought the company needed another round of investment. The chairman wasn't so sure.

The chairman's nephew had written his Harvard Business School thesis on the company. After handing in his essay, he was so worried about the business that he sold all of his shares. The chairman read his nephew's paper and refused to go along with Seabury's plan to invest even more. But Seabury won out.

He poured millions into the company. It didn't work. The textile industry in Massachusetts was failing. Nothing Seabury did helped. Depressed, he started drinking heavily. Cowin found this out, too and reported it to Buffett. They decided it was time to go for the throat. Buffett bought even more stock.

Seabury saw Buffett's new round of buying as a threat. He responded to Buffett's growing shareholding by making several offers to buy back Buffett's stock. This was one of the exits Buffett had thought about before he started buying. When Seabury's latest buyback pushed the stock price to $10, Buffett decided to travel to New Bedford. He wanted to meet Seabury and talk about his plans for another buyback.[20]

When they met, Seabury asked, "We'll probably have a tender [for our own stock] one of these days, and what price would you sell at, Mr. Buffet?"

Buffett responded, "I'd sell at $11.50 a share on a tender, if you had one."

Seabury said, "Well, will you promise me that if we have a tender you'll sell?"

Buffett replied, "If it's in the reasonably near future, but not if it's in twenty years from now."

"Fine," agreed Seabury.

Soon afterward, Seabury sent a letter to Buffett and the other shareholders offering to buy back stock at $11 3/8.

The amount was 12.5 cents per share less than Buffett and Seabury had agreed. Buffett was furious. He decided he wouldn't sell his position back to Seabury and Berkshire. He'd take it over instead. And he would pay more than $11 3/8 to do it.

Buffett moved quickly. First, he went to Otis Stanton to make an offer for his stock. Otis agreed to sell out to Buffett on one condition: Buffett had to make the same offer to Seabury. Buffett gladly agreed. Otis's shares pushed Buffett's shareholding to 49 percent, bought at an average price of $15 per share. That was enough to control the board.

Buffett then called a special meeting of Berkshire shareholders and was elected a director in April 1965. Seabury and his son Jack resigned at a board meeting a month later. The board elected Buffett chairman, a position he has held since. The stock closed that day at $18.

The *New Bedford Standard-Times* ran a story about the takeover. Remembering his earlier fight with the townsfolk of Beatrice and its local paper, Buffett said he would not liquidate. He assured the paper he planned to run the business.

Buffett did slowly liquidate Berkshire's textile business. When he got control, textiles were Berkshire's only business. Rather than reinvest Berkshire's earnings in textiles as Seabury would have, Buffett directed them to new businesses. The textile business just wasted away. He finally shut it down in 1985.

In his letter to the shareholders of Berkshire that year, Buffett wrote, "Should you find yourself in a chronically leaking boat, energy devoted to changing vessels is likely to be more productive than energy devoted to patching leaks:"[21]

Unless you are a liquidator, that kind of approach to buying businesses is foolish. First, the original "bargain" price probably will not turn out to be such a steal after all. In a difficult business, no sooner is one problem solved than another surfaces—never is there just one cockroach in the kitchen.

Second, any initial advantage you secure will be quickly eroded by the low return that the business earns. For example, if you buy a business for $8 million that can be sold or liquidated for $10 million and promptly take either course, you can realize a high return. But the investment will disappoint if the business is sold for $10 million in ten years and in the interim has annually earned and distributed only a few percent on cost. Time is the friend of the wonderful business, the enemy of the mediocre.

American Express

Buffett met Charlie Munger in 1959. Munger had a huge effect on Buffett's investment style over the years. Until he met Munger, Buffett thought about valuation only in terms of hard numbers. He said he wanted the figures to hit him over the head with a baseball bat. Munger thought Buffett was too limited.

Some businesses were "worth paying up a bit to get in with for a long-term advantage," he said.[22] When analyzing an investment, Munger thought more about its softer qualities. He tried to get Buffett to think about more than just the hard numbers.

The problem as Munger saw it was that the stocks

Buffett liked usually owned bad businesses. Munger didn't like bad businesses. "The trick," according to Munger, "is to get more quality than you pay for in price."[23]

Buffett's first step down Munger's road was an investment in American Express, or AmEx, as it is known. In 1963, AmEx was pulled into the "salad-oil" fraud committed by a client, Tino De Angelis. De Angelis bought and sold soybean oil, which he stored in tanks in his New Jersey warehouse.

AmEx is best known for its Traveler's Cheques and credit cards. But it also had a smaller business issuing *warehouse receipts*. (The documents are proof a client owns a commodity like soybean oil stored in a warehouse.) Warehouse receipts make it possible to *trade* a commodity like soybean oil—sell it back and forth—without moving the physical oil.

AmEx gave De Angelis warehouse receipts for the amount of soybean oil they thought was in his tanks, which De Angelis used to get margin loans against the oil and trade it.

What the AmEx inspectors didn't know was that De Angelis had not filled the tanks with soybean oil. He had tricked them into thinking he owned more soybean oil than he did by partially filling the tanks with seawater. De Angelis was so good at fooling the inspectors that they thought he owned more soybean oil than there was in the whole world.

De Angelis was caught when the price of soybean oil plunged and he couldn't pay his broker. The drop was so deep it wiped out De Angelis and his broker, too. Folks who had lent money against De Angelis's warehouse receipts looked to AmEx to pay them back. They complained AmEx should have made sure the tanks contained soybean oil and not seawater. It was a good argument. They wanted $175 million, which was more than ten times what AmEx earned in 1964. It looked like AmEx would be wiped out, too. The market cut the stock price in half.

Buffett became interested when he saw the stock price fall. AmEx was a tough stock to value. It was an insolvent lending business tangled in a fraud. Buffett wasn't worried about the fraud or the $175 million payment. He was worried about how AmEx's business customers viewed its credit. If they became apprehensive, they might stop taking traveler's cheques and AmEx cards. Restaurants and small hotels could go out of business if AmEx was wiped out. If they stopped accepting the cards, AmEx was finished. Buffett was also worried that De Angelis's fraud would stain AmEx's brand in the minds of AmEx cardholders. If it did, people might stop using the AmEx cards.

Buffett asked his broker, Henry Brandt, to find out if restaurants and other small businesses were still accepting AmEx. This was an unusual question from Buffett. He was usually only interested the hard data. Brandt staked out banks, restaurants, and hotels.

Brandt delivered to Buffett a foot-high pile of papers. Buffett read them with relish. He also visited several restaurants in Omaha. He saw they still accepted the card. The fraud hadn't hurt AmEx's brand. Buffett guessed AmEx would survive.

Buffett used about 40 percent, or $13 million, of his hedge fund to control just 5 percent of AmEx's stock. It was the largest bet the fund had ever made on a single company. With assets of just $32 million, Buffett Partners was too small to get control of AmEx. It could only ever be a general. If the stock price fell, Buffett couldn't keep buying. Two years passed.

In 1965, AmEx paid De Angelis's lenders $60 million, $115 million less than first sought. Buffett's gamble on AmEx paid off. The stock had traded below $35. Now it quickly popped to $49 per share. Buffett was up 40 percent in two years on his biggest shareholding.

The key to Buffett's change of heart was what happened next. Over the following five years, AmEx traded up to around $185. Its business continued to grow, and Buffett's hedge fund's holding grew with it. Buffett sold out when he liquidated the hedge fund in 1969. After five years, the shares were up more than five times.

The AmEx investment showed him Munger was onto something. Buffett knew it was worth at least $50 per share if it survived the salad oil crisis. But AmEx's value was not in its assets; it was in its business. And that business kept growing. Combining a growing business with a bargain price meant great returns that kept going year after year.

Munger was right. A good business bought at the right price was the better investment. There would be no more hostile control situations for Buffett. The returns were higher, but the stocks were too small for his growing bankroll. And the companies didn't grow.

Buffett said, "Charlie shoved me in the direction of not just buying bargains, as Ben Graham had taught me. This was the real impact he had on me. It took a powerful force to move me on from Graham's limiting view. It was the power of Charlie's mind."[24]

4. BUFFETT'S WONDERFUL COMPANIES AT FAIR PRICES

"It's far better to buy a wonderful company at a fair
price than a fair company at a wonderful price."
—Warren Buffett, "Chairman's Letter" (1989)

When Buffett heard See's Candies was for sale, he said,
"Call Charlie."[25] Munger lived in California. He knew all
about See's. He told Buffett, "See's has a name that no one
can get near in California…It's impossible to compete with
that brand without spending all kinds of money."[26] Buffett
looked at the numbers. He agreed he "would be willing to
buy See's at a price."[27]

The offering price was sky high. Harry See, the son of
the founder, wanted $30 million for a business with just $8
million in hard assets. The extra $22 million on top of the
hard assets bought See's *intellectual property*—its brand,
trademarks, and goodwill. And it bought a business that
earned $2 million after tax in 1971.

Buffett hesitated; $30 million was a lot of money. But
Munger argued See's was worth paying up for, so Buffett
countered with $25 million. At that price, Buffett and
Munger would pay 12.5 times See's profits and 4 times See's
hard assets. It was a huge leap for an investor who liked to

buy stocks at a fraction of hard asset value.

Harry See didn't want to lower his price, but Buffett explained that he and Munger were at the "exact dollar limit of what they were willing to pay."[28] Any higher and they would walk. See caved. On January 31, 1972, Buffett and Munger bought See's Candies for $25 million.

Why was Buffett willing to pay so much? He saw the value in See's *customer franchise*. See's chocolate was especially high quality. Chocolate lovers preferred it to candy that cost two or three times as much. Also, the customer service in See's shops was "every bit as good as the product."[29] It was "as much a trademark of See's as is the logo on the box."[30]

Together, these qualities created See's customer franchise. See's took cheap raw materials—sugar, cocoa beans, and milk—and turned them into premium chocolate. It earned the high margin between the raw material inputs and the branded chocolate output.

In the past, Buffett would have sought a lower price, perhaps a discount to the hard assets, to give a margin of safety. But See's ability to make lots of profit on little hard assets made it worth a lot more than its hard assets. See's high profits allowed it to grow quickly and throw off cash at the same time. But what was See's worth?

See's made just less than $5 million pretax in 1971. It earned a huge 60 percent profit on its $8 million in hard assets ($5 million ÷ $8 million = 60 percent). Let's assume a discount rate of between 10 and 12 percent. (In 1972, we could get 6 percent leaving our cash in the bank. We add on a little extra—4 or 6 percent—because See's is riskier than a bank account.) In that case, See's was worth between five and six times its hard assets (60 percent ÷ 10 or 12 percent = 5 or 6 times). With $8 million in hard assets, See's was worth between $40 and $48 million (5 or 6 × $8 million).

The $25 million price was only about one-half to two-thirds See's value. In this light, See's was a bargain. There is a secret to See's. Even if Buffett had paid full price, See's would still have been an incredible investment. Here's why.

In 2007, twenty-five years after Buffett bought it, See's earned $82 million on $40 million in hard assets. That was an amazing 195 percent return on assets. The huge growth in profit—from $5 million to $82 million—happened without much more invested in its hard assets.

See's paid out to Buffett almost all the profit it made between 1972 and 2007: $1.4 billion. And See's invested only $32 million to grow its hard assets ($40 million − $8 million = $32 million). Buffett got to use most of See's $1.4 billion in profit to buy other high-profit businesses for Berkshire.

This is why Buffett described See's as "a dream business." He compared See's to an ordinary business. He guessed an ordinary business needed about $400 million in hard assets to make the same $82 million profit as See's. Buffett means an ordinary business earns about 20 percent on its assets ($82 million ÷ $400 million = 20 percent). That's very high. And it would still be worth less than See's.

In 1989, Buffett summarized the lesson he learned from See's into a sentence: "It's far better to buy a wonderful company at a fair price than a fair company at a wonderful price." He continued, "Charlie understood this early; I was a slow learner."[31]

The Buffett Berkshire Strategy

"It is our job to select businesses with economic

characteristics allowing each dollar of retained earnings to be translated eventually into at least a dollar of market value."

—Warren Buffett, "Chairman's Letter" (1982)

With See's, Buffett moved beyond Graham's idea of value investing. Buffett still tried to buy stocks at a big discount from value, but he worked out that value differently. Graham saw the value in the hard assets and tried to buy them at a discount. Buffett saw the hard assets being only as valuable as the business's ability to profit on them. The higher the profit on assets, the higher the value of the business.

For example, let's say we have two businesses, each earning $1 million in profit. One has $5 million in assets. That's the *good* business. The other has $20 million in assets. That's the *bad* business. We can invest in the good business, we can invest in the bad business, or we can leave our money sitting in long-term bonds.

Return on Capital: High Profitability Is Worth More

The good business earns 20 percent on its $5 million in capital ($1 million ÷ $5 million = 20 percent). The bad business earns 5 percent on $20 million ($1 million ÷ $20 million = 5 percent). The long-term bonds yield 10 percent. What are the businesses worth?

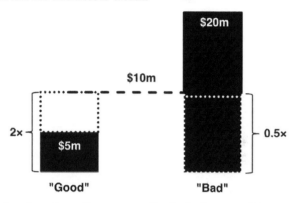

Valuation: Low Return on Capital Means a Discount

The good business is worth twice (20 percent ÷ 10 percent = 2 times) its assets, for example, 2 × $5 million = $10 million. This is because we get the same return from the long bond by investing twice as much.

The bad business earning 5 percent on invested capital is worth half its capital (5 percent ÷ 10 percent = 0.5 times). We calculate it's worth 0.5 × $20 million = $10 million because we can get the same return from the long bond— $1 million—by investing half as much.

Both businesses are worth $10 million. (And both have the same price-to-earnings (PE) multiple: 10 times.) Graham might have preferred the bad business at half its tangible asset value. But Buffett prefers the good business at twice its asset value. Why?

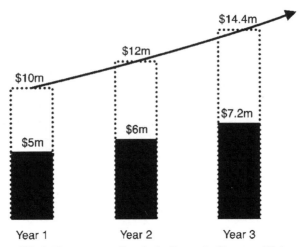

High Return on Capital: Growth Creates Value

Growth. Each dollar of profit reinvested in the good business is worth 200 cents on the dollar in business value (20 percent ÷ 10 percent = 2 times). Let's say the good business reinvests all its $1 million in profit and keeps up its 20 percent profitability. The next year, it will earn $1.2 million on $6 million in capital. Applying the same multiple, it is worth $12 million. Last year, it was worth $10 million. The $1 million reinvested in the business is worth $2 million in business value. Next year, it will be worth $14.4 million and so on.

Contrast this with the return to the owner of the bad business. Each dollar reinvested there becomes fifty cents on the dollar in business value (5 percent ÷ 10 percent = 0.5 times). The bad business chews up half of any dollar invested in it. How?

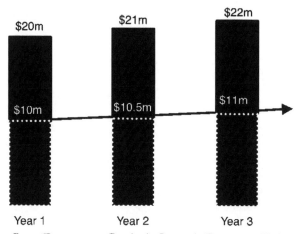

Low Return on Capital: Growth Destroys Value

Let's say the bad business reinvests all its $1 million in profit and maintains its profitability. The next year, it will earn $1.05 million on $21 million in capital. Valued the same way, the business is worth $10.5 million, just $500,000 more than the last year. The $1 million reinvested in the bad business is worth just $500,000 more in business value. It turned $1 in profit into 50 cents in value. Its growth destroyed value.

This is the most surprising result of Buffett's theory of value. Not all growth is good. Only businesses earning profits better than the rate required by the market should grow. Businesses with profits below that rate turn dollars in earnings into cents on the dollar in business value.

The owner of the good business wants the business to reinvest and grow because that growth is profitable. The owner of the bad business wants all the earnings paid out because the *growth* destroys value.

Alas, good businesses can't absorb much extra capital without profits going down. And bad businesses need all earnings reinvested just to keep up with inflation.

For a business to be worth more than its invested capital, it must maintain a profit greater than the market requires. In our earlier example, the market required 10 percent. For most businesses, high profits aren't sustainable because they attract competitors. While they may earn more over a short time, most businesses will only earn a market return—say 10 percent—on average over the full business cycle. Recall our earlier drawing of the business cycle:

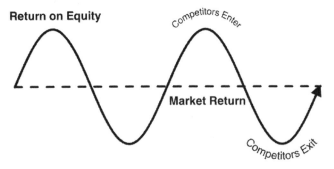

Business Cycle: High Returns Mean Revert Down

This, says Buffett, is why the moat is so important to the business:[32]

A truly great business must have an enduring "moat" that protects excellent returns on invested capital. The dynamics of capitalism guarantee that competitors will repeatedly assault any business "castle" that is earning high returns. Therefore a formidable barrier such as a company's being the low-cost producer (GEICO, Costco) or possessing a powerful worldwide brand (Coca-Cola, Gillette, American Express) is essential for sustained success. Business history is filled with "Roman Candles," companies whose moats proved illusory and were soon crossed.

In his Berkshire letters, Buffett has written a lot about moats. Buffett wants special businesses with a moat that resist mean reversion. He calls these "economic franchises."

This is how Buffett separates an economic franchise from an ordinary business: [33]

An economic franchise arises from a product or service that: (1) is needed or desired; (2) is thought by its customers to have no close substitute and; (3) is not subject to price regulation. The existence of all three conditions will be demonstrated by a company's ability to regularly price its product or service aggressively and thereby to earn high rates of return on capital. Moreover, franchises can tolerate mismanagement. Inept managers may diminish a franchise's profitability, but they cannot inflict mortal damage.

In contrast, "a business" earns exceptional profits only if it is the low-cost operator or if supply of its product or service is tight. Tightness in supply usually does not last long. With superior management, a company may maintain its status as a low-cost operator for a much longer time, but even then unceasingly faces the possibility of competitive attack. And a business, unlike a franchise, can be killed by poor management.

The economic franchise is a special business that earns high profits. Crucially, it keeps up profits over the business cycle despite the efforts of competitors. Competition causes the profits of an average business—one with no moat—to revert to the mean. Franchises resist mean reversion.

Franchises: High Returns Resist Mean Reversion

Most businesses can do no better than earn a market return. In peak years, they look like good businesses. In trough years, they look like bad businesses.

Good managers maximize a business's return on invested capital. Buffett recognizes, however, that there are limits to what management can do:[34]

> Good jockeys will do well on good horses, but not on broken-down nags…I've said many times that when a management with a reputation for brilliance tackles a business with a reputation for bad economics, it is the reputation of the business that remains intact.

This is Buffett's wonderful company, which earns defensible high returns on capital. It has good economics and resists competition. Good managers maintain the high returns by paying out any capital not needed in the business. They always work to shore up the moat.

The standard wonderful company—think See's Candies—grows with little extra capital and at a high rate while paying out most of its profits.

As long as the business earns high profits, wonderful companies pay investors to hold them for the long term. As Buffett quips, "When we own portions of outstanding businesses with outstanding managements, our favorite holding period is forever."[35] This allows the investment to compound without paying capital gains tax. It is one of the main reasons wonderful companies are good investment prospects.

With this leap made, Buffett left Graham behind. Graham warned it was too hard to tell whether high profits were due to good economics or a peak in the business cycle. "Corrective forces," Graham said, "are usually set in motion which tend to restore profits where they have disappeared, or to reduce them where they are excessive in relation to capital."[36]

Buffett heeded Graham's warning, but he believed some businesses could earn high returns due to their unusual economics. They could resist Graham's corrective forces.

In 1989, Buffett boiled down the investment lessons he had learned over thirty years after meeting Munger into a single sentence:[37]

It's far better to buy a wonderful company at a fair price than a fair company at a wonderful price.

A year later, at sixty, he would be a billionaire. In the next chapter, we look at an easy way to find Buffett's wonderful companies at fair prices.

5. HOW TO BEAT THE LITTLE BOOK THAT BEATS THE MARKET

"The market, like the Lord, helps those who help themselves. But, unlike the Lord, the market does not forgive those who know not what they do. For the investor, a too-high purchase price for the stock of an excellent company can undo the effects of a subsequent decade of favorable business developments."
—Warren Buffett, "Chairman's Letter" (1982)

In 2006, Joel Greenblatt published *The Little Book That Beats The Market*, where he promised an easy way to find Buffett's wonderful companies at fair prices. Greenblatt is a well-known value investor. He had great returns in his Gotham Capital fund over twenty years, and he has a long history of researching and writing about value investment. Greenblatt is now a professor at Columbia University. His *Little Book* described a test he ran on Buffett's wonderful companies at fair prices.

Greenblatt read through Buffett's Berkshire letters. He broke down Buffett's method into its two parts:

1. A wonderful company
2. A fair price

A Wonderful Company

> "I'd rather have a $10 million business making 15 percent than a $100 million business making 5 percent. *I have other places I can put the money.*"
> —Warren Buffett to Ken Chace, President, Berkshire[38]

Buffett says a wonderful company is one with a high return on equity. What does he mean? Return on equity measures how much money a company makes—the profit—for each dollar invested in it—the equity. The higher the profit on each dollar invested in the company, the more wonderful it is.

Here's an example. Let's say we have two businesses selling soft drinks: the Red Soda Company and the Blue Soda Company. Both sell bottled sodas from vending machines. The companies are identical except for the name and the color of the bottle.

$$\frac{\text{Wonderful}}{\text{Company}} = \frac{\text{Operating Earnings}}{\text{Equity}}$$

They have the same number of vending machines and a bottling plant where the soda is put in the bottles. They also each own a delivery truck to move the soda from the factory to the machines. They each spent the same amount of money—$10 million—building the factory, trucks, and machines. They both raised the $10 million in equity selling stock to the public, which was used to buy the $10 million in assets.

Soda drinkers prefer red sodas to blue sodas. Red Soda sells more sodas at a higher price than Blue Soda. At the end of the year, Red Soda has made $2 million in *operating earnings*. (Operating earnings estimate the income flowing to the owners of a company before any tax or interest is paid.

We will talk about it in some detail in the next chapter.)

Blue Soda has made just $1 million in operating earnings. Red Soda has earned a 20 percent return on equity ($2 million ÷ $10 million = 20 percent). Blue Soda has returned half as much, just 10 percent on equity ($1 million ÷ $10 million = 10 percent). Red Soda is more wonderful than Blue Soda because it made twice the return on equity. Simple.

A Fair Price

The second part of Buffett's rule is a fair price. For this, Greenblatt used what he called the "earnings yield."[39] We call it the Acquirer's Multiple. To avoid confusion, we'll call it the Acquirer's Multiple here. In the next chapter, we'll look at it in detail. It is a little like the PE multiple, which compares a company's market cap to its earnings—its profit. The PE multiple is a great rule of thumb to figure out how cheap a company is. The lower the multiple, the cheaper the company.

The Acquirer's Multiple works the same way, but it includes more data than the PE multiple. Stocks with low Acquirer's Multiples tend to do better than stocks with low PE multiples over time. The Acquirer's Multiple works better than the PE multiple because it is better at working out a stock's true price and its true earnings.

We'll examine the Acquirer's Multiple in some detail in the next chapter. For now, know the Acquirer's Multiple measures how much you have to pay for each dollar a company makes. The less you have to pay for the operating earnings, the better the price. Let's go back to Red Soda and Blue Soda.

We already know Red Soda made $2 million and Blue

Soda made $1 million in operating earnings last year. If we pay the same amount for each company, say $10 million, the Acquirer's Multiple will be 5 for Red Soda ($10 million ÷ $2 million) and 10 for Blue Soda ($10 million ÷ $1 million).

Red Soda is cheaper than Blue Soda because its Acquirer's Multiple at 5 is lower than Blue Soda's Acquirer's Multiple at 10. This is true even though we pay the same amount for each, $10 million. A lower Acquirer's Multiple means we get more operating earnings per dollar spent on shares of Red Soda.

The Magic Formula

Let's put the return on equity and the Acquirer's Multiple together. Greenblatt is looking for a stock that makes a lot of profit for each dollar invested in it. At the same time, he wants to pay as little as possible for each dollar it makes. He wants a wonderful company at a fair price.

Magic Formula = Wonderful Company + Fair Price

If we have the choice of investing in Red Soda or Blue Soda, we prefer Red Soda. Why? Because it has a higher return on equity (20 percent versus 10 percent for Blue Soda) and a lower Acquirer's Multiple (5 versus 10 for Blue Soda). Red Soda is more wonderful and at a fairer price than Blue Soda.

In 2005, Greenblatt asked a young computer programmer graduate of the Wharton school to test his Robo-Buffett. The Wharton grad told the computer to look at the biggest 3,500 stocks in a database of US financial data going back to 1988.

In each year, the program gave each stock in the database a rank out of 3,500 based on its Acquirer's

Multiple. It also gave each stock another rank out of 3,500 based on its return on equity. It added each stock's Acquirer's Multiple rank to its return on equity rank to create a new combined rank for each stock.

If we return to the Red Soda and Blue Soda examples, Red Soda gets a rank of 1 out of 2 for its Acquirer's Multiple because it is lower. Blue Soda gets a rank of 2 out of 2 because it has a higher Acquirer's Multiple. Blue Soda also gets a rank of 2 out of 2 for its return on equity because it is lower. Red Soda gets a rank of 1 out of 2 because it has a higher return on equity.

If we add Blue Soda's 2 out of 2 for the Acquirer's Multiple and 2 out of 2 for the return on equity, its combined rank is 4 (2 + 2). Red Soda's 1 out of 2 for the Acquirer's Multiple and 1 out of 2 for the return on equity gives it a combined rank of 2 (1 + 1). Red Soda's combined rank of 2 is lower than Blue Soda's combined rank of 4, so Red Soda is the better stock. We agreed that was true before, so this is a good system.

Greenblatt's computer program did the same thing but for all 3,500 stocks. It put together a portfolio of the thirty stocks with the best combined rank—the lowest Acquirer's Multiple and highest return on equity. It then tracked the portfolio's return over the next twelve months. It did that once a year for each of the seventeen years in the database.

When the testing was finished, Greenblatt looked at the results. He found them "quite satisfactory."[40] He called the combined wonderful-company-at-a-fair-price strategy the Magic Formula.

Testing the Magic Formula

We updated Greenblatt's research for this book. We

started our test in 1973 and tested each of the forty-four years until 2017. Greenblatt's portfolios of thirty magic formula stocks would have made 16.2 percent per year. To put this in context, investing at 16.2 percent per year for forty-four years would have turned $10,000 into over $7.6 million (before costs and taxes). Over the same time, the S&P 500 returned just 7.1 percent each year. The market would have turned the same $10,000 into just $205,481. There's no question, Greenblatt's Robo-Buffett is a great success.

The smallest company in Greenblatt's 3,500 stock database had a market cap of just $50 million in 2005. What about bigger companies? In 2005, Greenblatt limited the database to the largest 2,500 stocks. The smallest company had a market cap of $200 million in 2005.

The average yearly return went up to 17.2 percent, which was more than double the market's return. In a database limited to the largest 1,000 stocks, the smallest company had a market cap around $1 billion in 2005. The Magic Formula returned of 16.2 percent yearly on average. These are great results.

$10,000 Invested in the S&P 500 and Magic Formula (1973 to 2017)

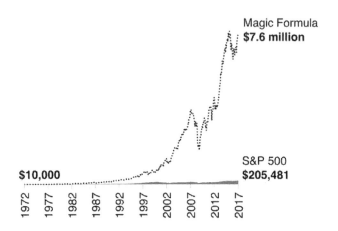

Magic Formula
$7.6 million

S&P 500
$205,481

$10,000

1972 1977 1982 1987 1992 1997 2002 2007 2012 2017

Thirty Stocks with Market Cap $1 Billion and Above

These tests of Greenblatt's Magic Formula show it would have beaten the market by a wide margin.

If most highly profitable businesses mean revert to lower profits, why do Magic Formula stocks beat the market? Is it buying a mix of Buffett's wonderful businesses and some fair businesses at a cyclical peak? What if we remove the need for high profits and just buy undervalued companies using the Acquirer's Multiple? What if we buy fair companies at wonderful prices?

6. THE ACQUIRER'S MULTIPLE

"In the old legend the wise men finally boiled down the
history of mortal affairs into the single phrase,
'This too shall pass.'"
—Benjamin Graham, *Security Analysis* (1934)

The Acquirer's Multiple is an industrial-strength PE
multiple. It's a throwback to the corporate raiders and
buyouts of the 1980s. In dusty, old finance journals, it is
described it as the Acquirer's Multiple because corporate
raiders and buyout firms—the acquirers—used it to find
whole companies cheap enough to take over. Where most
investors only look at profits, the corporate raiders looked
to see what a company owned. They used it to find treasure
hidden in plain sight on corporate balance sheets.

The Acquirer's Multiple compares the total cost of a
business to the operating income flowing into the company.
It assumes the acquirer can sell assets, pay out the
company's cash, or redirect the business's cash flows.

It is a powerful tool because it reveals hidden cash and
hidden cash flows. It also uncovers hidden traps and
companies carrying huge debt loads.

The Acquirer's Multiple is the *enterprise value* divided by *operating earnings*.

$$\text{Acquirer's Mulitple} = \frac{\text{Enterprise Value}}{\text{Operating Earnings}}$$

Think of the enterprise value as the price you pay and operating earnings as the value you get. The lower the Acquirer's Multiple, the more value you get for the price you pay and the better the stock. Let's look at each of the parts: enterprise value and the operating earnings.

Enterprise Value: How to Buy a Stock for Free

The enterprise value is an x-ray into the company. It is the total price an acquirer of a company must pay. What's the difference between the enterprise value and the market cap?

Market cap tells us how much it costs to buy all of a company's shares. It is the number we would arrive at if we counted all of a company's shares and multiplied it by the stock price.

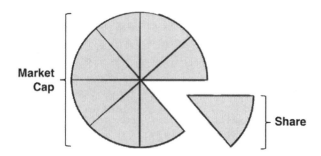

Market Cap and a Share: Pizza and a Slice

The relationship of share price and market cap is easy to

visualize as a pizza. Market cap is the whole pizza, and each share is a slice. If we don't know how many slices are in the pizza, the price of a piece tells us nothing about the price of the whole pie.

Pies the same size can be cut into four, eight, or sixteen pieces or more. We need to know the price of each piece of pizza—each share—and the number of pieces in the pie—shares on issue—to know the total price—market cap.

For example, if the share price is $10, and there are 8 million shares on issue, the market cap is $80 million ($10 per share × 8 million shares). Market cap goes up and down with the stock price. If the stock price goes up to $20, the market cap goes up to $160 million ($20 per share × 8 million shares). If the stock price goes down to $5, the market cap goes to $40 million ($5 per share × 8 million shares).

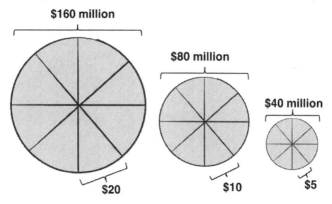

Market Cap and Share Prices: Up and Down

The market cap will also go up and down with the number of shares on issue. If the company issues more stock, the market cap will go up. If the company buys back stock, the market cap will go down. Even if we're only going to buy a few shares and not the whole company, we should think about the whole company. Doing so makes us aware of share issues and buybacks.

Some new investors make the mistake of thinking the price of a share tells us how expensive the company is. They think a $10 share is twice as big or expensive as a $5 share. This isn't right. Until we know how many shares are on issue, we don't know which company is bigger or more expensive.

Let's say the company with $10 shares has 4 million shares on issue. The other company with $5 shares has 8 million shares on issue. Both companies have the same market cap of $40 million ($10 × 4 million and $5 × 8 million = $40 million). (And we still don't know which is more expensive. We still have to compare what we're paying with what we're getting.)

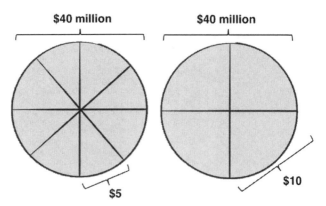

Market Cap, Shares, and Prices: How Many?

To know the total price of a company's stock, we must know both its stock price and the number of shares on issue. This is the market cap. But it's not the whole story.

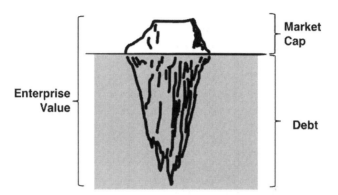

Enterprise Value: The Whole Iceberg

Enterprise value tells us how much it costs to buy all of the stock and all of the debt (and other things like debt). It's like looking at an iceberg. Market cap is the bit poking above the water. It's easy to see. It's the rest of the iceberg under the waterline—the debt—that sinks big ships. That's why we look there, too. Sometimes we find good news; the company has lots of cash and no debt. That makes it cheaper than it appears.

Let's say we have two stocks that are the same in every way but one. Both have a market cap of $10 million. One has $5 million in debt, and the other has $5 million of cash in its bank account and no debt. Which one is cheaper? The company with $5 million in cash is cheaper than the one with $5 million in debt. But we can't tell from the market cap alone. Both have an identical market caps of $10 million. Why is the company with $5 million in cash cheaper than the company with $5 million in debt? Let's look at what happens when we acquire all of the shares of each company.

If we spend $10 million buying the company that owes $5 million in debt, we now own a company with $5 million in debt. We have to service the debt. What we can take out of the company will be cut by the cost to carry the debt until we pay it off. What about the company with $5 million in cash? If we spend $10 million buying that company, we can immediately use the cash and any profits. The company only cost us $5 million because we got the cash back.

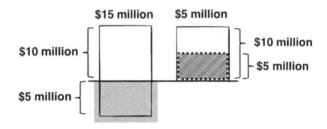

Enterprise Value: Debt is Bad and Cash is Good

How would the enterprise value treat these two companies? The enterprise value penalizes the company with debt by adding the debt onto the market cap. It rewards the company with cash by taking away the cash from the market cap. The company that owes $5 million in debt has an enterprise value of $15 million ($10 million in market cap + $5 million in debt). The company with $5 million in cash has an enterprise value of $5 million ($10 million in market cap – $5 million in cash).

Why is debt important? Let's use General Motors (GM) as a real-life example. In 2005, GM had a market cap of $17 billion and debt of $287 billion. If we only looked at GM's market cap, we would have missed its huge pile of debt. Adding the debt to GM's market cap gave an enterprise value of at least $304 billion. Using GM's enterprise value would allow us to see it was a lot bigger than its market cap suggested. When GM filed for bankruptcy in 2009, its huge pile of debt was a major reason.

The enterprise value includes two other important costs that are like debt: preferred stock and minority interests.

Preferred stock is stock that pays its holder a preferred dividend. (It is *preferred* because it is paid before the common stock dividend and has some other rights the common stock doesn't have. If the company doesn't have enough money to pay both, it can only pay the dividend on the preferred stock.)

It is like debt because the dividend is fixed and must be paid regularly, just like interest. The enterprise value penalizes companies with preferred stock by adding the preferred stock on to the market cap. A company with a $10 million market cap and $10 million in preferred stock has an enterprise value of $20 million ($10 million + $10 million = $20 million).

A minority interest is a small stake in a company's business owned by someone else. If we own all of a company and someone else owns 10 percent of the business, we only own 90 percent of the business. To own all of the business, we have to negotiate with the other party to buy out his or her minority interest. Enterprise value treats the minority interest as another debt. It must be paid by an acquirer of the whole company, just like debt or preferred stock.

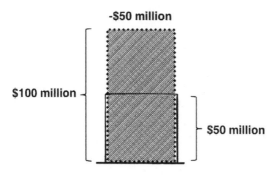

Negative Enterprise Value: Extra Cash Is Great

Companies with enterprise values of $0 (and less) do

exist. A low or negative enterprise value is a good thing to find. It means the company has little debt and lots of cash relative to the market cap.

The market is telling stocks with negative enterprise values the business is worth less than nothing. If you buy a stock with a negative enterprise value, you are being paid—indirectly—to buy the stock. You could use the company's own cash to buy all of its shares. In practice, stocks with low or negative enterprise values often (but not always) own bad businesses. They burn lots of cash.

For example, let's say a company has a $50 million market cap and $100 million in cash. It has an enterprise value of –$50 million ($50 million – $100 million = –$50 million). Companies with negative enterprise values attract activists who can redirect the cash to other uses. They can liquidate the business and pocket the cash leftover after paying all the costs.

As we learned with GM, an enterprise value much bigger than the market cap might suggest the company has a lot of debt (or preferred stock or minority interests). It is more expensive than it appears by looking at market cap alone. This is why we say the enterprise value is the true price of a company.

Operating Earnings

In his letters to shareholders, Warren Buffett often writes that he tracks "operating earnings before interest and taxes." At Berkshire, he says his "main focus is to build operating earnings."[41] So what are operating earnings?

Buffett says, "The 'operating earnings' of which we speak here exclude capital gains, special accounting items and major restructuring charges."[42] Operating earnings is the income that flows from a business's operations. It leaves out interest and taxes. It also leaves out unusual, one-off things like gains from selling an asset or settling a lawsuit. The one-off items are left out because they won't occur again in the future. They don't show the usual operations of the business.

Operating earnings are not reported in a company's financial statements. They must be worked out from them. They are defined follows:

Operating Earnings =
   Revenue
   - Cost of Goods Sold
   - Selling, General, and Administrative Costs
   - Depreciation and Amortization

If we compare the earnings number reported by a company—the bottom line—to its operating earnings, the difference between the two will be interest and taxes. When working out operating earnings, we add back interest and tax because interest is tax-deductible. The amount of interest a company pays on its debt affects the amount of tax it pays.

Operating earnings are very similar to *earnings before interest and taxes* or *EBIT*. Many times, the numbers will be identical. But operating earnings differ from EBIT because the operating earnings figure is worked out from the top of the income statement down, and EBIT is worked out from the bottom up. Calculating operating earnings from the top down standardizes the metric, making a comparison across companies, industries, and sectors possible. By excluding *special items*—income that a company does not expect to recur in future years—ensures that these earnings are related only to operations.

Investors use operating earnings to make an apples-to-apples comparison between stocks. For example, let's say we have two identical companies, but one has a lot of debt, and the other has none. The company with a lot of debt will pay a lot of interest, and its tax will be lower. It will have a lower net income. The company with no debt will pay no interest and more tax. It will have a higher net income.

Adding back the interest and tax allows us to compare the earnings of the two companies. When we do, we will see the businesses made the same operating earnings. They are identical, so they should be worth the same amount. Operating earnings allows an apples-to-apples comparison between stocks with different mixes of debt and equity.

How To Use The Acquirer's Multiple

If we divide a stock's enterprise value by its operating earnings, we get its Acquirer's Multiple. How do we use it? Like the PE multiple, we can compare two different companies to see which is cheaper. The lower the multiple, the better. An Acquirer's Multiple of 5 is cheaper than an Acquirer's Multiple of 10. Let's look at some examples.

Let's say we have two companies. The first has a market cap of $10 million, $5 million in cash and operating earnings of $1 million. It has an enterprise value of $5 million ($10 million − $5 million). It has an Acquirer's Multiple of 5 ($5 million ÷ $1 million).

The second has a market cap of $10 million, $5 million in debt and operating earnings of $1 million. It has an enterprise value of $15 million ($10 million + $5 million). It has an Acquirer's Multiple of 15 ($15 million ÷ $1 million).

The first company with the lower Acquirer's Multiple is cheaper. This is true even though the companies have the same size market cap ($10 million each) and operating earnings ($1 million each). The debt and cash makes the difference.

How do we decide between a stock on an Acquirer's Multiple of 20 and a bank account earning 5 percent? Are they comparable? Roughly. Operating earnings aren't directly comparable to interest because we can't spend them. We can spend interest. Remember, we have to account for any debt the company has. The interest payments will affect the tax paid and the net income the company makes.

The Acquirer's Multiple is best for comparing two or more companies. And that's how we use it. We work it out for every company listed on the stock market. Then we look for the most deeply undervalued—those with the lowest Acquirer's Multiple.

How does the Acquirer's Multiple stack up against the Magic Formula?

7. THE SECRET TO BEATING THE MARKET

"A fact, once logically arrived at, should not be extended beyond its natural significance."
—John Le Carré, *A Murder of Quality* (1962)

In 2017, I asked Euclidean Technologies, Inc. to run an independent test of the Acquirer's Multiple and the Magic Formula. Euclidean is a quantitative value-investment firm based in Seattle, Washington, run by Michael Seckler and John Alberg, who are pioneers in the application of machine learning to equity analysis. Euclidean has developed one of the best databases of financial data for research in the United States.

Euclidean simulated portfolios of thirty stocks from 1972 to 2017. Portfolios of Acquirer's Multiple stocks were compared to portfolios of Magic Formula stocks and the market. Euclidean ran the test in each of Greenblatt's three universes: stocks with a market caps bigger than $50 million, $200 million, and $1 billion. The results are stunning. (For details on the simulation, see the appendix.)

Market Cap $50 Million And Above

$10,000 Invested in Acquirer's Multiple, Magic Formula, and S&P 500 (1973 to 2017)

In our $50 million market-cap test, the Acquirer's Multiple beat the Magic Formula. Both beat the S&P 500. The Acquirer's Multiple compounded at 18.6 percent yearly. The Magic Formula managed a respectable 16.2 percent yearly.

That small advantage to the Acquirer's Multiple made a big difference over the full forty-four years. A theoretical $10,000 invested in each strategy became $18.7 million for the Acquirer's Multiple and $7.6 million for the Magic Formula.

Market Cap $200 Million And Above

$10,000 Invested in Acquirer's Multiple, Magic Formula, and S&P 500 (1973 to 2017)

In our $200 million market-cap test, the Acquirer's Multiple also beat the Magic Formula but by a smaller margin. Again, both beat the S&P 500. In the larger universe, the Acquirer's Multiple compounded at 17.5 percent yearly. The Magic Formula averaged 17.2 percent annually.

That tiny advantage to the Acquirer's Multiple made a little difference over the full forty-four years. A theoretical $10,000 invested in each strategy became $12.6 million for the Acquirer's Multiple and $11.2 million for the Magic Formula.

Market Cap $1 Billion And Above

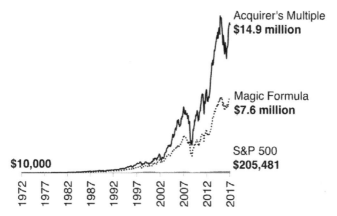

**$10,000 Invested in Acquirer's Multiple, Magic
Formula, and S&P 500 (1973 to 2017)**

Finally, in our biggest $1 billion market-cap test, the
Acquirer's Multiple beat the Magic Formula by a wide
margin. Both beat the S&P 500. In the biggest universe, the
Acquirer's Multiple compounded at 17.9 percent yearly. The
Magic Formula averaged 16.2 percent annually.

That small advantage to the Acquirer's Multiple made a
big difference over the full forty-four years. A theoretical
$10,000 invested in each strategy became $14.9 million for
the Acquirer's Multiple and $7.6 million for the Magic
Formula.

In each universe chosen by Greenblatt, the Acquirer's
Multiple beat the Magic Formula. (For more detail on the
simulated returns, refer to the appendix.)

What caused the Acquirer's Multiple to beat the Magic
Formula? Mean reversion. Choosing stocks on historical
profitability reduces returns. To show it, we created a new

strategy that only buys stocks with the highest profits. It doesn't look at value. We call it *Pure Charlie* in honor of Charlie Munger's Poor Charlie from *Poor Charlie's Almanac*.

Pure Charlie is the opposite of the Acquirer's Multiple. He is pure profit and is all about return on invested capital. He buys the thirty stocks with the highest profits. He doesn't care about value at all. Here's how Pure Charlie stacks up to the Acquirer's Multiple and the Magic Formula in the same test.

Market Cap $50 Million And Above

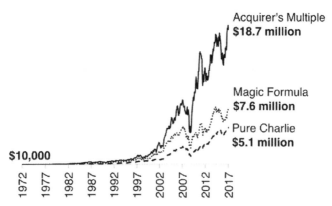

$10,000 Invested in Acquirer's Multiple, Magic Formula, and Pure Charlie (1973 to 2017)

In our $50 million market-cap test, both the Acquirer's Multiple and the Magic Formula beat out Pure Charlie. Notably, Pure Charlie still beat the market. (It's not a bad strategy.) Pure Charlie managed a reasonable 15.1 percent yearly. Over the full forty-four years, a theoretical $10,000 invested in Pure Charlie became $5.1 million.

Market Cap $200 Million And Above

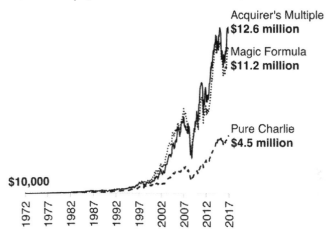

$10,000 Invested in Acquirer's Multiple, Magic Formula, and Pure Charlie (1973 to 2017)

In our $200 million market-cap test, both the Acquirer's Multiple and the Magic Formula again beat out Pure Charlie, who returned 14.8 percent yearly. Pure Charlie beat the market again. Over the full forty-four years, a theoretical $10,000 invested in Pure Charlie became $4.5 million.

Market Cap $1 Billion And Above

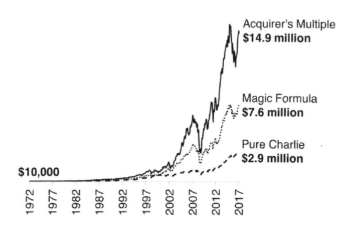

Acquirer's Multiple
$14.9 million

Magic Formula
$7.6 million

Pure Charlie
$2.9 million

$10,000

1972 1977 1982 1987 1992 1997 2002 2007 2012 2017

$10,000 Invested in Acquirer's Multiple, Magic Formula, and Pure Charlie (1973 to 2017)

In our biggest $1 billion market-cap test, both the Acquirer's Multiple and the Magic Formula beat out Pure Charlie. Pure Charlie returned 13.7 percent yearly. Pure Charlie still beats the market. Over the full forty-four years, a theoretical $10,000 invested in Pure Charlie became $2.9 million.

Pure Charlie is not a bad strategy. Buying portfolios of highly profitable companies works. But it doesn't beat the Magic Formula, which looks at value, too. Of course, looking purely for value works best. That's why the Acquirer's Multiple beats both. (For more detail on the simulated returns, please refer to the appendix.)

These results aren't unusual. Dresdner Kleinwort, an investment bank, found the same thing in the United Kingdom and Europe in a test from 1993 to 2005.[43] The Acquirer's Multiple beat the Magic Formula in each of those places over the same time. Only in Japan did the Magic Formula give the Acquirer's Multiple a run for its money.

Dresdner Kleinwort found chasing wonderful companies shrinks returns. The gains from using the Acquirer's Multiple by itself are "sizeable." The best they said for the Magic Formula was that it would have helped the Acquirer's Multiple keep up with the market in the dot-com bubble. Undervalued stocks fell behind in the frothy boom from 1997 to 1999. The Dresdner Kleinwort paper concluded, "In general we find that the value strategy is very powerful."

There is also a 2009 paper by Loughran and Wellman on the enterprise multiple, a close relative of the Acquirer's Multiple. It concluded the enterprise multiple was a "highly significant measure of relative value…for virtually the entire universe of US stocks":[44]

> In other words, our results may actually be relevant to both Wall Street and academics.

Why does the Acquirer's Multiple beat the Magic Formula? Why do fair companies at wonderful prices beat wonderful companies at fair prices? An older study by Greenblatt holds a clue.

Greenblatt's Cigar Butts

"Our statistical screens are merely exploiting a group of undervalued stocks that are easily identified and are further protected by strong balance sheets and large asset values. Additionally, because of the depressed nature and liquid make-up of the companies that meet our test criteria, they are often the object of takeover initiatives."
—Joel Greenblatt, "How The Small Investor Beats The Market" (1981)

In 1976, nineteen-year-old Joel Greenblatt read about Benjamin Graham for the first time. He read a *Forbes Magazine* article called "Ben Graham's Last Will and Testament." It described an interview Graham gave to the *Financial Analysts Journal* just months before his death in 1976.

In the article, Graham said he was no longer in favor of complicated ways of valuing stocks. All that he needed were a few simple tools.

The important idea was to buy a group of stocks meeting some simple yardstick for undervaluation. Graham said he would pay little mind to each stock.

Graham suggested investors use his cigar-butt method, the same method Buffett used in his hedge fund to find Sanborn Maps and Dempster Mills. This method looks for stocks with more cash and other liquid assets than debt. Then it buys only those stocks at a big discount to the net value. Graham said it was "foolproof" and "unfailingly dependable."[45]

Greenblatt was a student at the Wharton School when he read the article. He was intrigued. He decided to test Graham's method. With his classmates Rich Pzena and Bruce Newberg, Greenblatt read through a pile of old Standard and Poor's stock guides. The three wanted to figure out the returns to Graham's cigar-butt stocks.

They decided to test the returns through a time of big market moves. They chose the volatile six years from April 1972 through April 1978, which included the 1974 stock market crash when the market almost halved. It also included the strong recovery that saw the market double.

They had to value each stock and track its returns by

hand. It was a big job. They limited the study to stocks starting with the letters A or B that were bigger than $3 million.

This sample included about 750 stocks. That was about 15 percent of the stocks listed in the Standard and Poor's stock guides. After months of painstaking testing, Greenblatt, Pzena, and Newberg had some results. They found Graham's cigar butts beat the market by a lot, more than 10 percent each year.

Greenblatt wrote up the results. The article appeared in the *Journal of Portfolio Management* in 1981 and was called "How the Small Investor Can Beat the Market."

In the article, Greenblatt, Pzena, and Newberg asked, "Why does it work?" They answered, "We were unable to discover any 'magic' qualities associated with stocks selling below liquidation value":[46]

> Simply stated, by limiting our investments to stocks that according to fundamental notions of stock valuation appear severely depressed, we were able to locate more than our share of these inefficiently priced, undervalued securities. In other words, there are probably many more undervalued stocks that are not selling below liquidation value.

Graham was right. Buying a group of stocks using his simple cigar-butt rule worked. Other studies confirm Greenblatt's results.

In 1983, Henry Oppenheimer tested Graham's cigar-butt rule again. Oppenheimer was then an associate professor of finance at the State University of New York. He looked at the returns over thirteen years from 1970 to 1983. Oppenheimer found the rule beat the market.

With Jeffrey Oxman and Sunil Mohanty, we tested Graham's cigar-butt rule over twenty-five years from 1983 to 2008. We found it beat the market, too. Why does it work?

First, the stocks are undervalued. And the more undervalued they are, the bigger the return. Graham's instinct about the margin of safety is right. The greater the discount, the bigger the gain.

For each stock, Oppenheimer worked out the discount to its cigar-butt value. He put the stocks into five groups, from the most undervalued to the most expensive. The most undervalued group beat the next group and so on. The most expensive group had the lowest returns. The most undervalued group beat the most expensive group by more than 10 percent a year.

Oppenheimer's second finding is his most interesting one. He split the stocks into two groups. One had only profitable stocks, and the other, only loss makers. Oppenheimer found the loss makers beat the profitable group.

His third finding is also interesting. He split the profitable group again. The first group was comprised of dividend-paying stocks. The second group paid no dividend. Oppenheimer found the stocks that didn't pay a dividend beat the ones that did.

We agreed with Oppenheimer. Cigar butts beat the market. Loss-making cigar butts beat profitable ones. Cigar butts that didn't pay a dividend beat those that did. Why?

In short, mean reversion.

We expect to find the wider the discount to value, the better the return. The other findings are unexpected. But both fit our theory of mean reversion.

Mean reversion pushes up the beaten-down prices of undervalued stocks. It pushes up beaten-down businesses, too.

The key to maximizing returns is to maximize our chance at mean reversion. That means maximizing the margin of safety. We want the most undervalued stocks. And we want to make sure they survive to mean revert.

A wide margin of safety is important because it gives mean reversion time to work its magic. Here are some simple rules we can take from the Acquirer's Multiple and Graham's cigar-butt studies to maximize the margin of safety.

The Secret: Margin of Safety

In *Security Analysis*, Graham wrote that if asked to "distill the secret of sound investment into three words," he would say "margin of safety."

We find the margin of safety chiefly in the discount to value. But it is also a test of the balance sheet and the business. Here are three rules covering the margin of safety:

1. The greater the company's discount to its value, the bigger the margin of safety. The bigger the margin of safety, the better the return and the lower the risk. A wide discount allows for the ordinary errors in calculations of value, and it allows for any drop in value.

This breaks the received wisdom of the market.

And financial academics ignore it. Both think higher returns mean more risk.

2. Find a margin of safety in a company's balance sheet. Many, many stocks have sunk due to too much debt. We need to make sure the stocks have more cash than debt or that the debt is small relative to the business. The Acquirer's Multiple favors exactly these stocks.

3. Find a margin of safety in a company's business. The company should own a *real* business, which should have historically strong operating earnings with matching cash flow, which confirms the accounting earnings are real. It means they are not the creation of a clever embezzler's mind. We should also look for signs of earnings manipulation. This can be the first step down the road to fraud.

Companies that own science experiments or toys in search of a business model are for speculators. But weak current profits in a stock with a good past record creates a good chance for deep-value contrarians to zig.

8. THE MECHANICS OF DEEP VALUE

"Above all, he liked it that everything was one's own fault. There was only oneself to praise or blame. Luck was a servant and not a master. Luck had to be accepted with a shrug or taken advantage of up to the hilt. But it had to be understood and recognized for what it was and not confused with a faulty appreciation of the odds, for, at gambling, the deadly sin is to mistake bad play for bad luck. And luck in all its moods had to be loved and not feared."
—Ian Fleming's James Bond, *Casino Royale* (1953)

Michael J. Mauboussin has studied what makes wonderful businesses stay wonderful. He is the head of global financial strategies at investment bank Credit Suisse. Like Greenblatt, he's also an adjunct professor of finance at Columbia Business School. He's written four books on value investing and behavioral finance. In 2012, he published a fantastic book called *The Success Equation*, where he looks at what happens to great businesses over time.

Why do fair companies at wonderful prices beat wonderful companies at fair prices? Because great businesses don't stay great. They only look great at the top of their business cycle. Mean reversion pushes great business back to average.

Remember that a great business is one that is unusually profitable. It makes more money for each dollar invested in it than other businesses. Mauboussin finds that as time goes on, most highly profitable businesses see profits fall until the businesses become average. A tiny handful keep profits up, but we don't know how they do it. We can't tell the few that can maintain high profits from the many that become average. It's random chance.

Mauboussin showed how unusually high or low profits trend toward the average by tracking one thousand companies from 2000 to 2010. He ranked the businesses on *economic profit*—how wonderful each was—in the year 2000.[1] He put them into five groups. The top group was the most profitable. These were the great businesses. He put the bad businesses in the bottom group. These, on average, lost money.

The chart below shows the results. For each of the five groups, there is a clear trend toward average profits. The

---

[1] Economic profit is calculated as ROIC – WACC. "ROIC" stands for "Return On Invested Capital." It's another name for return on equity or return on capital. ROIC measures how much money a business makes for each dollar invested in it. The more it makes, the better it is. "WACC" stands for "Weighted Average Cost of Capital." It measures the rate the market charges a business for its capital. On debt capital it is the interest rate. On equity capital it is the expected return set by the market. The market charges riskier firms more, and safer firms less. In practice, this means riskier firms should expect a lower PE, and safer firms a higher PE. The difference between ROIC and WACC is economic profit. This analysis recognizes that capital isn't free. A business is only wonderful if it makes a profit beyond its cost of capital, or, in other words, an economic profit.

highly profitable companies become less profitable. The loss makers lose less money. All trend toward average profitability.

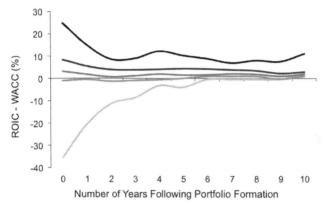

Mean Reversion: Profit Trends Toward Average

Source: Michael J. Mauboussin, *The Success Equation: Untangling Skill and Luck in Business, Sports, and Investing.* (Boston: Harvard Business Review Press), 2012.

The reason great businesses become average businesses is mean reversion. Things go back to normal. It means profits move back toward the average over time. A great business is an outlier. It is more profitable than average. Over time, competitors eat away the unusually high profits until the business earns average profits.

This also happens to bad businesses, which are less profitable than average. Over time, competitors leave the industry until the businesses that stay earn average profits. This is the machinery of mean reversion.

Some businesses do keep up oddly high profits. Mauboussin found a tiny handful of stocks kept high profits from start to finish. But he could not find the reasons why. And he couldn't find the things that predict which businesses will keep up high profits. All he could say for sure is that some businesses stay highly profitable, while most go back to average.

Warren Buffett can pick the needles from the haystack. He can find these companies with "moats" that protect them from competitors. Without the moat, competitors storm the gates and push the high returns back toward the average. Few companies have a moat. Even most seemingly great companies don't have one. For this reason, most highly profitable companies see profits fall over time.

Here is the simple truth: profits move toward the average over time. Only some stocks avoid it, and we don't know why. Without Buffett's genius for business analysis, we can't rely on a high-profit business staying that way. This is why fair companies at wonderful prices beat wonderful companies at fair prices.

Straight-Line Errors

"Our statistical screens are merely exploiting a group of undervalued stocks that are easily identified and are further protected by strong balance sheets and large asset values. Additionally, because of the depressed nature and liquid make-up of the companies that meet our test criteria, they are often the object of takeover initiatives."
—Joel Greenblatt, "How The Small Investor Beats The Market" (1981)

Werner De Bondt and Richard Thaler are economists who study investor behavior and stock prices. They are known as behavioral economists. In 1987, De Bondt and Thaler had an idea. Stocks get undervalued or expensive because we overreact. Mean reversion is likely. But we "extrapolate" the profit trend too far. We draw a straight line through the recent profits and assume the trend keeps going.

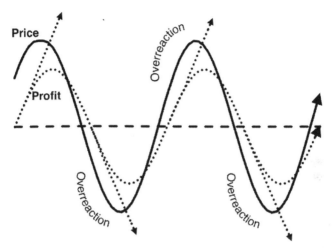

Overreaction: The Profit Trend Extrapolated Too Far

Investors expect stocks with profits that have gone up for a few years to keep going up. And they think stocks with a few years of falling profits will keep going down.

Stocks with rising profits get expensive because investors expect the profits to keep going up. And stocks with falling profits become undervalued because investors expect the earnings will keep falling. In other words, investors don't expect profits to mean revert. But they're wrong. Mean reversion is the likely outcome.

De Bondt and Thaler tested the idea by finding undervalued and expensive stocks and then tracking the profits. They ranked groups of stocks by price-to-book value.

Book value is the value of a company's assets (what it owns) less its liabilities (what it owes). It is one measure of a company's value. Price-to-book value measures how much you pay for that value. If you pay less than book value, you may be getting a bargain. If you pay more than book value, you may be overpaying.

De Bondt and Thaler put the stocks into five groups. We'll call the cheapest group the *undervalued* stocks. They called the expensive group the *expensive* stocks.

The chart shows the change in earnings per share for the undervalued and expensive stocks in the three years leading up to the date they're picked.

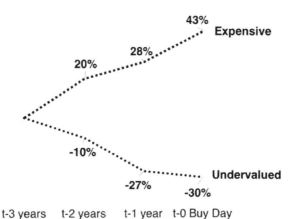

t-3 years   t-2 years   t-1 year   t-0 Buy Day

Overreaction: Profit Trend before Buying (1966–1983)

Data Source: Werner F. M. De Bondt and Richard Thaler. "Further Evidence on Investor Overreaction and Stock Market Seasonality," *The Journal of Finance* 42, no. 3 (1987), 557–581, doi:10.2307/2328371.

It's easy to see why the undervalued stocks were undervalued. Profits fell 30 percent in three years before they were picked. Investors expected those profits to keep falling.

Expensive stocks were expensive because profits had

risen 43 percent in the same three years. Investors expected the earnings to keep rising. Let's see what happened next.

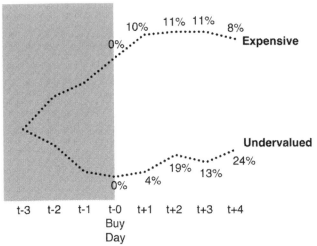

Mean Reversion: Profit Trend after Buying (1966–1983)

Data Source: Werner F. M. De Bondt and Richard Thaler. "Further Evidence on Investor Overreaction and Stock Market Seasonality," *The Journal of Finance* 42, no. 3 (1987), 557–581, doi:10.2307/2328371.

Stunning. After they were picked, the profits of the undervalued stocks went up more than expensive stocks. The undervalued stocks' earnings rose 24 percent in the next four years. (The chart is incredible evidence of mean reversion in earnings.)

The expensive stocks' earnings growth slowed to 8 percent over the same time. The expensive stocks couldn't maintain the earlier profit growth. The undervalued stocks delivered better profit growth. This is mean reversion in action.

The undervalued stocks also delivered better stock price returns. They beat the market by 41 percent over four years.

Meanwhile, the stocks in the expensive portfolio *lagged* the market by 1 percent. These are striking results.

De Bondt and Thaler's findings are good evidence of mean reversion in profits. Big increases and decreases in profits don't continue for long. Stocks get undervalued because we expect the profit trend to continue. Instead, mean reversion kicks in.

The big declines turn into growth. And fast growth slows down. As a result, undervalued stocks' profits go up faster than expensive stocks' profits.

Undervalued stocks' prices go up more than the market, too. If we want high profit growth and a stock price that goes up faster than the market, we should look at undervalued stocks.

In Search of Unexcellence

Tom Peters's 1982 bestseller, *In Search of Excellence*, is described as "the greatest business book of all time." In the book, Peters looked at 43 of America's best-run companies to find out what made them "excellent." The companies had high profitability and growth. Peters has a doctorate from Stanford. He described himself as an "ex-engineer" with a vague idea that "numbers and statistics weren't enough."

> We suspected that they didn't tell the whole story
> about how companies really worked.

The book promised the "eight basic principles of management...that made these [companies] successful." It was a huge hit.

Five years later, analyst Michelle Clayman took another look at the stocks Peters branded *excellent*. She found most of the businesses had weakened. The high growth and profits had disappeared. In fact, most of the stocks were no longer excellent by Peters's own rules. The reason? Mean reversion. Competition had pushed the high profits and growth rates back to the average. She said:[47]

> In the world of finance, researchers have shown that returns on equity tend to revert to the mean. Economic theory suggests that markets that offer high returns will attract new entrants, who will gradually drive returns down to general market levels.

Peters's excellent companies disappointed as investments, too. As a group, they lagged the stock market. Individually, two-thirds lagged the market and only one-third beat it. Clayman said the excellent stocks lagged because the market thought future growth and profit would be higher still. As a result, they got too expensive.

Using the same rules as Peters, Clayman went "in search of disaster." She created a portfolio of *unexcellent* stocks. The table below shows Clayman's unexcellent stocks beside a new group of excellent ones picked using Peters's rules.

Peters's "Excellent" Stocks versus Clayman's "Unexcellent" Stocks (1976 to 1980)

	Excellent	Unexcellent
Asset Growth	22%	6%
Return on Equity	19%	7%
Price-to-Book Value	2.5×	0.6×

The excellent stocks were much better than the unexcellent stocks on every measure but one: valuation. Growth was higher for the excellent stocks at 22 percent per year. The unexcellent stocks grew at just 6 percent per year.

The excellent stocks also had a better return on equity: 19 percent. The unexcellent stocks returned just 7 percent. (Remember, high return on equity is what makes businesses "wonderful.")

If you only looked at asset growth and return on equity, you might expect the excellent stocks to beat the unexcellent stocks. But Clayman's excellent stocks were undervalued, and the excellent stocks were expensive.

Clayman's unexcellent stocks traded at 0.6 times book value. Peters's excellent stocks traded at 2.5 times book value. In other words, the unexcellent stocks were fair companies at wonderful prices, and the excellent stocks were wonderful companies at fair prices. Which stocks were the better investment?

In 2013, Barry B. Bannister tested Clayman's unexcellent stocks from June 1972 to June 2013. Bannister found the unexcellent stocks beat the excellent stocks and the market by a wide margin. The unexcellent stocks averaged 14 percent per year, while the excellent stocks returned only 10 percent per year. Over the same time, the market averaged 11 percent.

The unexcellent stocks beat the market by 3 percent per year, and the excellent stocks did not. The excellent stocks lagged the market by 1 percent per year.

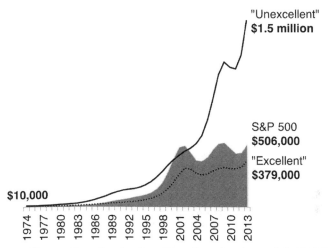

"Unexcellent"
$1.5 million

S&P 500
$506,000

"Excellent"
$379,000

$10,000

1974 1977 1980 1983 1986 1989 1992 1995 1998 2001 2004 2007 2010 2013

Unexcellent Stocks Beat Excellent Stocks and S&P 500
Data Source: Barry B. Bannister and Jesse Cantor. "In Search of "Un-
Excellence"—An Endorsement of Value-style Investing" Stifel Financial Corp.
July 16, 2013..

The chart shows the value of $10,000 invested in the
unexcellent stocks. The same amount was also invested in
the excellent stocks and the stock market. The returns were
tracked from June 1972 to June 30, 2013.

The reason the unexcellent stocks beat the excellent
stocks and the market? Mean reversion. According to
Bannister:[48]

> In theory, high returns invite new entrants that drive
> down profitability, while poor returns cause
> competitors to exit, as well as lead to potential new
> management or acquisition by a competitor or
> financial buyer.

The excellent stocks lagged because their businesses
worsened. The profitability and asset growth trended to the
average. The businesses of the unexcellent stocks also

worsened but not as much as the excellent stocks. Clayman's unexcellent stocks beat the market because the discount between price and value closed. In other words, the price-to-book values went up.

The unexcellent stocks' price-to-book value trended to the average, and the stock prices went up. The excellent stocks stayed better businesses than the unexcellent stocks. But the excellent stocks' valuation went down, so the stock price of the excellent stocks lagged. This is mean reversion.

Mean reversion means the stock prices of undervalued stocks are likely to rise over time, and the stock prices of expensive stocks fall.

Profitable industries attract competition. The same forces push out competitors in loss-making industries. For this reason, wonderful businesses tend to be fair investments, and fair businesses tend to be good investments.

Wonderful stocks lag because investors overestimate future growth and profits. Fair businesses beat the market because investors underestimate the change in the stocks' price-to-value ratio. Undervalued stocks trend toward the average value, and the price rises. Expensive stocks trend toward the average value, and the price drops.

Expecting mean reversion is good investing. It works on growth rates, returns on equity, and stock prices. This leads to two rules central to good value investing:

1. Over time, undervalued stocks beat expensive stocks and the market. The reason? Stock prices mean revert to value. Expensive stocks go down. Undervalued stocks go up. This is why value investors like Icahn and Buffett beat the

market.

2. Returns on equity and earnings growth rates mean revert, too. High returns on equity go down. High rates of earnings growth slow. Low returns on equity rise. Low or negative earnings growth improve.

This is why fair companies at wonderful prices beat wonderful companies at fair prices and why the Acquirer's Multiple tends to beat the Magic Formula.

Contrarian investors take advantage of mean reversion. They know undervalued stocks with low returns on equity or falling profits beat the market. They know glamor stocks with high returns and growth lag the market.

Buffett knows this, too. That's why he is careful to buy companies with moats. The Magic Formula does not know this. The Acquirer's Multiple doesn't, either. But it pays much less for operating earnings than the Magic Formula, which causes it to beat the Magic Formula.

The Acquirer's Multiple is the best of both worlds. It looks for deeply undervalued stocks. And some of them will be compounders given time.

Are there investors who seek out fair companies at wonderful prices? In the next chapters, we'll meet them. We'll see what they look for and how they find those targets.

9. THE PIRATE KING

"I have heard that on neutral ground he was incredibly
fierce, and affronted people by saying the most blunt or
even savage things. Certainly those who did not know him
well approached him with caution or heavily armed."
—Winston Churchill, *My Early Life: 1874-1904* (1930)

It is 1 a.m. on December 15, 1989. It is near the coldest
part of the night on one of the coldest days of the year in
the coldest December on record in New York. Thirty men
struggle to lift a seventy-one-hundred-pound statue from
the back of a flatbed truck. It is hard to move because it is
heavy and smooth, eighteen feet long and eleven feet high.
The men have to work fast. It is freezing cold, and they are
committing an act of vandalism.

They have less than eight minutes. In that time, the
patrolling New York police officers will be back. With the
help of a rented crane, the men lift the statue from the back
of the truck. They drop it into place under the sixty-foot
Christmas tree in the middle of Broad Street. It sits right in
front of the New York Stock Exchange. In five minutes, the
truck and all but one of the men drive away.

The last man is a forty-nine-year-old Sicilian immigrant, Arturo Di Modica. The sculpture is his. He has spent $346,000 of his own money and two years of his life to build it. It is a huge, muscular bronze bull, horned and scowling with its head down. It leans to its left, nostrils flared and tail whipped up over its back. Di Modica calls it *The Charging Bull.* Crafted in the wake of the 1987 stock-market crash, he says it is a reminder: a symbol of aggression, optimism, and wealth. It stands for the strength and power of the American people. It is his gift to the city of Manhattan.

Di Modica waits in the freezing cold for the sun to come up. Early-morning commuters are the first to discover it. He is delighted as people stop to stare at the huge bronze bull. A crowd builds. Hundreds of the city's workers and tourists stand around it, staring, and touching it. A line forms to rub its horns for good luck. A second, longer line forms to burnish its balls. Di Modica will watch until noon when he will break for lunch.

That afternoon, officials at the New York Stock Exchange will demand that it be removed. Di Modica doesn't have a permit. (He hasn't even tried to get one. This is guerilla art. You don't ask for permission. This for the people.) The police refuse the Stock Exchange's request. They are either unwilling or unable to move the three-and-a-half-ton bull. The next night, a private contractor will drag it away to an impound lot in Queens.

A photographer from *The New York Post* captures the moment the bull is hauled away on the back of another flatbed. The next day, the shot will appear under the headline, "Bah, Humbug! N.Y. Stock Exchange Grinches Can't Bear Christmas-Gift Bull. Leveraged Pry Out." New Yorkers are furious. The public outcry forces the New York City Department of Parks and Recreation to return the bull. Less than a week later, on December 21, 1989, the bull will be fixed at Bowling Green. It stands there today, an icon. Di Modica has pulled off the last takeover of the 1980s, the takeover decade.

The takeover decade actually kicked off in 1976 when Carl Icahn sent a short document to would-be investors for his new hedge fund. Dubbed *The Icahn Manifesto*, it set out Icahn's plan to find undervalued stocks and take them over.

Icahn said it was "a unique way to create large profit-making opportunities with relatively little risk:"[49]

> Most domestic companies and almost all foreign companies are loath to launch an "unfriendly" takeover attempt against a target company. However, whenever a fight for control is initiated, it generally leads to windfall profits for shareholders. Often the target company, if seriously threatened, will seek another, more friendly enterprise, generally known as a "white knight" to make a higher bid, thereby starting a bidding war. Another gambit occasionally used by the target company is to attempt to purchase the acquirers' stock or, if all else fails, the target may offer to liquidate.
>
> It is our contention that sizeable profits can be earned by taking large positions in "undervalued" stocks and then attempting to control the destinies of the companies in question by:
>
> a) trying to convince management to liquidate or sell the company to a "white knight";
>
> b) waging a proxy contest;
>
> c) making a tender offer and/or;

d) selling back our position to the company.

Icahn said the main problem was the managers of the target companies "generally own very little stock themselves and, therefore, usually have no interest in being acquired." He likened it to a gardener who stopped a homeowner from selling a house because the gardener might lose his job.

Icahn's plan was simple: first, acquire a stake in an undervalued company. The stake should be big enough to get management's attention. Second, push management to sell the company. At the same time, let the market know the stock is undervalued by starting a proxy fight to get control. If management won't sell, put the company "in play" by making a hostile takeover bid.

The takeover bid put Icahn in a win-win position. On one hand, it created a price floor in the stock. Icahn could wait to see if another buyer would make a higher bid and sell to them. If no other bidder emerged, Icahn could buy the company himself. He'd get it undervalued because no one else wanted it.

By trying to control the company, Icahn could control his own destiny. He could buy an undervalued stock and single-handedly force its price up to its value. Icahn wouldn't wait on mean reversion and the market to move up the stock price. He'd use Buffett's old *control situation* trick. And he'd do the heavy lifting himself.

Icahn's first target was Tappan Stove Company, an old range and oven maker founded in 1881. Icahn's analyst, Alfred Kingsley, brought the stock to his attention. Looking at the valuation, Kingsley later said:[50]

At the time we took our position in Tappan, everyone else was hot on Magic Chef, but I said, "The multiple on Magic Chef is too high. Where is it going to go from here?" Magic Chef was at the top of its cycle and Tappan was at the bottom. That's where I preferred to stake our claim.

Tappan was a small player in a market ruled by General Electric and Westinghouse. Icahn thought they might buy Tappan if he could put it in play.

Icahn started buying stock at $7.50. He pegged Tappan's value at around $20 per share. That made his upside around $12.50 per share ($20 − $7.50 = $12.50) or close to three times his investment ($20 ÷ $7.50 = 2.7 times). The big discount limited his downside and created a huge upside if he could get Tappan taken over. It was the perfect win-win target.

After Icahn bought his starting stake, he called Tappan's president, Donald Blasius. Icahn told Blasius he had acquired fifteen thousand shares and was thinking about buying more. Blasius didn't get the message. He thought Icahn was pleased he had taken the time to talk to him about Tappan.

Icahn was not pleased. He bought another fifty-five thousand shares and called Blasius again. This time, there would be no mistake. Icahn told Blasius he liked Tappan as a takeover candidate. He said he had made a lot of money buying undervalued stocks. Many times, a buyout had doubled the stock price. He thought Tappan was a good target for a takeover. Still, Blasius didn't understand what Icahn was telling him. Takeovers were rare in 1977.

Icahn upped his holding to several hundred thousand shares and stepped up his efforts to find a buyer for Tappan. He also continued buying Tappan stock. By late 1978, his position was big enough to file a 13D notice with the

Securities and Exchange Commission (SEC). A shareholder with more than 5 percent of a company's shares must file a 13D if they plan to take over or liquidate the company.

With the filing, Wall Street finally got the news that Tappan was in play. The stock price jumped. Icahn called Blasius to tell him an acquirer had called him wanting to buy his stock for $17. It was less than the $20 Icahn wanted, but he was thinking about selling. He also asked for a seat on the board. Blasius said no. Finally, he saw Icahn was a real threat.

The company moved to issue stock to block a hostile takeover. This created a problem for Icahn. The new stock would stop him from being able to use his shareholding to push for a sale of the company. He had to put a stop to the new stock issue.

Icahn responded by speaking to the press. He wanted to embarrass Tappan into withdrawing the stock issue and selling the company. It worked. The bad press made the board fold almost at once. They agreed to withdraw the stock issue.

Icahn pressed on. In April, he sent a letter to Tappan shareholders and wrote that he wanted a seat on the board. He also wanted to sell the company at his $20-per-share estimate of its value. It was a huge premium to its market price. He said the managers didn't care that the stock was down because they were paid too much. Icahn thought like an owner of the business. He wrote:[51]

> If I personally owned a business with these operating results and which had a substantial net worth, I would certainly seek to sell that business. I believe the same logic should apply in the case of Tappan.

He reminded the shareholders that the withdrawn stock issue had been to block a takeover. Icahn pledged that if he was elected to the board, he would quickly push to sell the company near its $20 value. The letter worked. Icahn won his seat on Tappan's board.

As a director, Icahn was as good as his word. He moved quickly to sell Tappan's assets. At the first board meeting, he pushed for the liquidation of the company's money-losing Canadian arm. It owned valuable real estate that could be sold. He also sold the factory in Anaheim, California.

At the same time, Icahn pressed for the sale of the entire company. He shopped Tappan to buyout firms and other potential acquirers.

Blasius saw Icahn had won and would shortly find a buyer for Tappan. He moved to find his own white knight, so he met with the giant Swedish appliance-maker AB Electrolux and offered to sell. Electrolux agreed and bid $18 per share.

It was a great result for Icahn. Electrolux's bid delivered him a $2.7 million profit on his 321,500 shares, almost 100 percent on his $9.60-per-share average price.

At the final board meeting to approve the sale to Electrolux, Tappan's chairman, Dick Tappan, said, "Icahn has done us a favor. We got a 50 percent premium over the company's market value, and Electrolux is going to make capital investments in Tappan."[52]

Tappan turned to Icahn and said, "If you have any deals you want to cut me in on—"

Icahn said, "Yes, I have one going on now."

It was Icahn's hedge fund. And so, Dick Tappan invested $100,000 in the Icahn Partners fund. As the table shows, it was a great investment.

Target Company	Three Months Prior To Attempt At Target	High After Attempt At Target
Tappan	$8	$18
Warner Swasey	$29	$80
National Airlines	$15	$50
Wylain	$13	$28 ½
Flintkote	$30	$55

Source: Mark Stevens, *King Icahn* (New York: Penguin Group, 1993).

From a humble start, Icahn grew into a "formidable raider and financial tactician," as his biographer Mark Stevens painted him.

At the peak of his power in the 1980s, Icahn controlled billions in capital. He attacked the giants of the public markets, which included Texaco, the "Big Red Star of the American Highway," for which he bid $12.4 billion. He also attacked U.S. Steel, the world's first billion-dollar corporation, then with a market cap of $6 billion.

Other investors took notice. A cottage industry of so-called *corporate raiders* sprang up. They disappeared with the 1987 stock market crash. But a new breed of activist investors emerged in the wake of the dot-com bust in the early 2000s. We'll learn about two in the next chapter.

10. NEW GENTLEMEN OF FORTUNE

"It seemed a very great world in which these men lived;
a world where high rules reigned and every trifle in public
conduct counted: a duelling-ground where although the
business might be ruthless, and the weapons loaded with
ball, there was ceremonious personal courtesy and mutual
respect."
— Winston Churchill, *My Early Life: 1874-1904*, (1930)

It is early September 2000, more than a decade since Di
Modica slipped his bull into Manhattan. The dot-com bust
started in March, but few feel it yet. After falling just over
10 percent in April, the market has almost rallied back to its
peak. But it won't regain the highs. A sickening 50 percent
plunge winds its way down the pike. The bear market won't
be official—down 20 percent—for another six months. For
now, the waters appear calm. But a young hedge fund
manager, Dan Loeb, has a big problem.

Loeb manages a hedge fund called Third Point Partners
from an office twenty-seven floors above Park Avenue in
Manhattan. He named Third Point after a surf break in Los
Angeles, where Loeb grew up. Thirty-three-year-old Loeb
launched Third Point in June 1995 with just $3.3 million

from family and friends. Only $340,000 of it was Loeb's.

He has grown that small grubstake at 35 percent every year since, turning every dollar invested with him into almost $5. Now, five years later, he runs $200 million.

His second-largest holding is animal-feed maker Agribrands. Loeb has put $22 million—more than 11 percent—of his fund into the stock. He paid around $40 per share for the stake. Now the company's chief executive, Bill Stiritz, plans to sell it for $39 per share, a dollar less than Loeb paid.

Sixty-five-year-old Stiritz is a wheeler-dealer. He was made chief executive of Agribrands's former parent, Ralston Purina, in 1981. At the time, it was a messy conglomerate. It owned an animal-feed business, a pet-food business, a fast-food chain, mushroom and soybean farms, a ski resort, and a pro ice hockey team.

Stiritz sold the Saint Louis Blues, the Keystone ski resort, the farms, the Jack in the Box restaurants, and the Purina Mills animal feed business. He bought some better businesses, folding in the makers of Twinkies and Eveready batteries.

All the deal-making paid off. Operating profit shot up 50 *times* under Stiritz's watch. At the same time, the company bought back so much stock that its shares shrunk 60 percent. The stock price, which traded at $1.25 when he took over in 1981, had vaulted into the $80s by the time he stepped down in 1997.

His final act at Ralston Purina was to spin off two businesses. The cereal and grocery business went into a company called Ralcorp. The international animal-feed business was spun off as Agribrands. Stiritz then stepped down to become both chief executive and chairman of Agribrands and also chairman of Ralcorp. Including the spin-offs, Stiritz created more than one hundred times the value he inherited.

Now, as chief executive and chairman of Agribrands, Stiritz plans to sell the business to Ralcorp, where he also serves as chairman. It makes sense to him. Ralcorp has better businesses. Agribrands has piles of cash. Stiritz yearns to repeat with Ralcorp his experience at Ralston Purina. Key is getting Agribrands's cash pile for cheap. The sales price is too low, which is great for Stiritz and great for Ralcorp, but bad for the shareholders of Agribrands and a big problem for Dan Loeb.

Third Point owns about 4 percent of Agribrands's stock. That doesn't give Loeb much pull. Stiritz won't take a call from such a small shareholder and certainly not from a guy with a fund named after a surf break in California. Stiritz is the hundred-bagger legend. Loeb is some punk kid. But Stiritz is in the wrong, and Loeb is right. Unfortunately, right and wrong doesn't count for much here. Influence is all that matters.

Loeb can't bend Stiritz to his will with anything less than 50 percent of Agribrands's shares. To buy that much stock, he would need another $190 million—$10 million more than he has in his fund. And he doesn't want to put all his chips on this one stock, anyway. Stiritz is intent on merging Agribrands's cashbox into Ralcorp's businesses at a big discount to its true value. And Loeb's little fund has a big problem.

Loeb remembers a stunt pulled by a hedge-fund-manager buddy of his, Robert L. Chapman Jr. Chapman and Loeb have been friends for a decade. Loeb even slept on Chapman's couch for a while when he was younger and between apartments. Chapman runs a hedge fund called Chapman Capital out of Los Angeles.

The 13D

Earlier in the year, Chapman got into a fight with another company, American Community Properties Trust. He was upset when a shakeup overseen by J. Michael Wilson, the thirty-two-year-old chairman and chief-executive son of the founder, led to a 40 percent slide in the share price.

With 5 percent of American Community's shares, Chapman had to file a Schedule 13D notice with the SEC, the stock market police. In the 13D, Chapman had to tell the market what he planned to do with his American Community stake. Would he try to take over American Community? Would he try to liquidate it? Would he try to sell it to someone else? Item No. 7 on the 13D asks for any "Material to be Filed as Exhibits." In a flash of inspiration, Chapman decided to attach an open letter to Wilson.

In the letter, Chapman wrote he invested in American Community because he thought it was a "highly undervalued microcap company."[53] (A *microcap* is a tiny company when measured by market cap.) The shakeup was supposed to boost the price of the shares. Instead, the stock had almost halved.

Only the Wilson family had done well. They had bought some assets from the company for less than they were worth. They had been paid huge salaries. Wilson senior had also been paid hundreds of thousands of dollars in consulting fees and payouts. Chapman described the shakeup as piling "strategic blunder on Wilson-family plunder."

He was also upset the company wouldn't return his phone calls. Chapman called the company three times a day, but the executives of American Community ignored most of his calls. The rare times they returned calls, they did so much, much later—weeks, months, or in one case, a year. Chapman wrote that Wilson was trying to push the share price down so the family could buy the company cheaply.

Chapman's plan was for the company to liquidate. He figured that would stop the Wilson-family "gravy train." And would return money worth almost seven times more than the share price. He signed off in a flourish. The board was letting a thirty-two-year-old "graduate of Manhattan College in the Bronx and former bank loan administrator" play a "real-life version of Monopoly."[54]

Very truly yours,
Robert L. Chapman Jr.

Chapman's letter worked. He publicly shamed Wilson and American Community into selling assets and paying down debt. American Community also started paying a dividend. Later, when asset sales slowed, Chapman started phoning Wilson again. His first seven phone calls were ignored.

When he finally got through, Wilson told Chapman, "You're a [expletive] pain in the ass, and we don't want to talk to you."[55] Chapman put the phone call in another SEC filing, which attracted a lot more attention from the media. The result? Wilson and American Community again sped up its sales. The stock soared.

Chapman's letter-writing campaign was a blunt instrument, but it got the job done. It attracted attention from the media and the market, and the stock jumped. Loeb figures it's just what he needs. He buys enough stock in Agribrands to push him over the 5 percent level. Now he can file a 13D with the SEC.

He still has no real power. But the 13D gives him a voice, and Loeb has a mouth. He used to pay a bigger kid a quarter a day to protect him when it got him into trouble in the schoolyard. Now he plans to use it to stir up some trouble for Stiritz. He will put Stiritz's plan under a spotlight.

Chapman had written his letter in high English like he'd swallowed a dictionary. He filled it with phrases like "tacitly dissuade," "egregious inefficiencies," "proffering," "efficacious means," "nepotistic practices," and "cognitive dissonance." A shareholder needed a degree in English literature to know what he meant.

That won't be a problem for Loeb. He's part of the new breed of investors trolling Internet message boards, posting rumors and *flaming* (insulting) one another. Loeb's screen name is "Mr. Pink," one of the main characters in Quentin Tarantino's bloody heist-gone-wrong film *Reservoir Dogs*. Mr. Pink gets away with the diamonds in the end.

In his letter to Stiritz, Loeb is open about what he's doing. He writes that he bought more stock only so that he could file the letter with the SEC. He believes it's the only way to get his "strong opposition…taken seriously and heard widely." He is angry the price offered for Agribrands is too low. As proof that the sale is too cheap, he points to Agribrands's Acquirer's Multiple and PE multiple. These are his tools in trade.

Tools of Titans

"Our experience has been that pro-rata portions of truly outstanding businesses sometimes sell in the securities markets at very large discounts from the prices

they would command in negotiated transactions involving entire companies."
—Warren Buffett, "Chairman's Letter" (1977)

Few investors had heard of the Acquirer's Multiple in the early 2000s. This is the age of venture capital, dot coms, and IPOs. Loeb uses the Acquirer's Multiple the way the corporate raiders used it: to reveal hidden cash, hidden cash flows, hidden traps, and companies carrying huge debt loads. He has used it to dig up Agribrands's hidden cash hoard—the same pile of cash Stiritz is trying to quietly slip into Ralcorp.

Ralcorp has offered $39 per share in cash or $420 million for all of Agribrands's shares. But Agribrands has $160 million in cash sitting in the bank, which Stiritz can use if he gets control. Stiritz is only paying $260 million for Agribrands ($420 million less Agribrands's $160 million in cash). Ralcorp will also have to pay out Agribrands's $10 million debt. It must be added to the $260 million for a total enterprise value of $270 million. Loeb sees that Ralcorp has offered only $270 million for Agribrands's business. What was Agribrands giving up for $270 million?

Ninety million dollars in operating earnings. Stiritz was offering just $270 million for Agribrands's $90 million. Dividing the $270 million enterprise value by the $90 million in operating earnings put Ralcorp's bid on an Acquirer's Multiple of 2.9 times, which was less than three years of cash flow from Agribrands's business. Too cheap by half. He works out the PE multiple by dividing the $420 million by $53 million in reported earnings, or 7.9 times. Again, way too cheap.

In his letter to Agribrands, Loeb writes that Ralcorp's $39 per share offer means an Acquirer's Multiple of 2.9 times and a PE multiple of 7.9 times. It is far too cheap.

He's a buyer at that price, not a seller. He wields the pen like a flamethrower. The sales price is too low, and the sale process is "unfair."[56]

As chairman of Ralcorp and chief executive and chairman of Agribrands, Stiritz is on both sides of the sale. He's "put[ting his] own personal interests ahead of the shareholders" and "strip[ping the] assets at an unfair price."[57] Loeb says that Agribrands's cash and cash flows belong to Agribrands's shareholders. They should not be used to "serve the empire-building desire of Ralcorp's management team." Loeb wants Agribrands put up for sale "to maximize shareholder value."[58]

Very truly yours,
Daniel S. Loeb

On December 4, 2000, three months after Loeb sends his letter, Agribrands announces that it will not sell to Ralcorp. Instead, Cargill, a privately owned processor of feed and agricultural products, will be the bidder. The price? $54.50 per share, $15.50 and 36 percent more than Ralcorp offered. It is a huge gain for Loeb's second-biggest holding. And it makes Loeb infamous.

Loeb will use the infamy to hammer out a niche for himself. He's the self-appointed sheriff on a frontier ignored by the media and the SEC. He will buy small shareholdings, just enough to file a 13D, and fire off a letter to management. Though the methods are seemingly mad, there's a method to the madness. The letters are flares shot into the darkness. And they work.

Loeb has captured the mood of the time. Investors ache for rebellion against remote boards of directors who believe they have the divine right of kings to sit on corporate boards. He is against those who do not answer to the earthly authority of shareholders and those who do not heed the consent of the people. Almost by accident, Loeb has stumbled onto the strategy that will make him a billionaire in just five short years.

Einhorn's Icahn Moment

Billionaire value-investor David Einhorn founded the hedge fund Greenlight Capital in 1996 with just $900,000. His parents invested two-thirds of the assets: $600,000. He has returned 25 percent per year since. Now he runs $9 billion and is worth $1.5 billion.

In early 2013, Einhorn pushed Apple, Inc., then trading at $60, to pay out some of its huge pile of cash. Einhorn said that Apple's $150 billion in cash was too much for a stock with only $60 billion in fixed assets. Apple could use it to buy "all but 17 companies in the S&P 500."[59] It earned next to no interest. It was better in the hands of shareholders.

He said Apple's stock price was discounted to the value of the cash, about $20 per share. Apple could "unlock significant shareholder value" by cutting the cash on its "bloated balance sheet."[60]

Einhorn wasn't the only activist to complain about Apple's cash pile. Carl Icahn wrote an open letter to Apple's chief executive, Tim Cook. Icahn asked for Apple to return cash through a $150 billion buyback. Icahn wrote in the letter:[61]

> When we met, you agreed with us that the shares are undervalued. In our view, irrational undervaluation as dramatic as this is often a short-term anomaly. The timing for a larger buyback is still ripe, but the opportunity will not last forever. While the board's actions to date ($60 billion share repurchase over three years) may seem like a large buyback, it is simply not

large enough given that Apple currently holds $147 billion of cash on its balance sheet, and that it will generate $51 billion of [operating earnings] next year (Wall Street consensus forecast…With such an enormous valuation gap and such a massive amount of cash on the balance sheet, we find it difficult to imagine why the board would not move more aggressively to buy back stock by immediately announcing a $150 billion tender offer (financed with debt or a mix of debt and cash on the balance sheet).

Icahn also sent this tweet to his Twitter followers:[62]

 **Carl Icahn** ⊘
@Carl_C_Icahn

We currently have a large position in APPLE. We believe the company to be extremely undervalued. Spoke to Tim Cook today. More to come.

RETWEETS **1,942**   LIKES **668**

11:21 AM - 13 Aug 2013

↩ 279   🔁 1.9K   ♥ 668

Icahn said a $150 billion buyback would boost earnings per share by 33 percent. It would also lift the share price 150 percent to $150. Why did Einhorn and Icahn fix on Apple getting value for its cash?

Activists focus on excess cash because too much can hurt a company's value. Let's take a look at Apple in 2013. It had a market cap of $500 billion. It earned $37 billion in net income over the preceding year and made $50 billion in operating earnings. It also carried $150 billion in cash. Let's also say the ten-year treasury bond offers a 3 percent yield. The table below summarizes Apple's financial data.

Apple, Inc.'s Summary Financial Data

Summary Balance Sheet	
Net Cash and Equivalents	$150 billion
Other Assets	$60 billion
Total Assets	$210 billion
Summary Income Statement	
Operating Earnings	$50 billion
Net Income	$37 billion
Other Statistics and Ratios	
Market Cap	$500 billion
Enterprise Value	$350 billion
PE Multiple	14×
Acquirer's Multiple	7×
Return on Equity	67%
10-Year T-Bond Yield	3%

The PE multiple for Apple was 14 ($500 billion ÷ $37 billion = 14 times). This is low for a good business. The PE multiple of the ten-year treasury bond was 33 times (1 ÷ 0.03). The ten-year treasury bond is an alternative investment to Apple. We can invest in the ten-year treasury at 33 times or Apple at 14 times. Apple is less than half the PE multiple of the ten-year treasury. It is the better bet.

Apple is even more interesting when we look at it with the Acquirer's Multiple. It trades on an Acquirer's Multiple of 7 ($350 billion ÷ $50 billion). Apple can return all of its huge pile of cash to its shareholders because it has strong operating earnings.

Einhorn noted that to work out the value this unlocks, we have to guess how much value the market already places on Apple's cash. If the market gives it no credit and it returns all its cash, then the cash returned is found value. This means the dividend unlocks the whole $150 billion or $20 per share.

This might occur if the return on assets is boosted to more than 83 percent ($50 billion ÷ $60 billion). Profitability like that justifies a PE multiple of 14 times or higher. In that event, the market cap would stay unchanged at $500 billion. Shareholders get $150 billion and keep stock with the same market cap, $500 billion. If the market already gives Apple some credit for the cash, the amount unlocked would be cut. Einhorn wrote:[63]

> There is no way to know for sure how much credit the market gives, so there is no way to know how much value will be unlocked. But the range is no less than zero and no more than [the value of the cash distributed].
>
> The caveat is that to the extent that this would reflect Apple adopting a better capital-allocation policy such that cash and future cash aren't trapped indefinitely, the market might reward Apple with a higher P/E ratio.

Late in 2013, Einhorn and Icahn succeeded in getting Apple to pay out most of its cash. It started a buyback. By February 2014, it had bought back $40 billion of stock, a record amount for any company over a twelve-month span. It then announced in 2014 that it would return $130 billion through an increased buyback and dividend.

The stock price leapt. After trading as low as $56 in May 2013, the 2014 announcement pushed the stock to $100. Icahn let the world know in a series of tweets:[64]

By the end of the year, it was at $120. Icahn scored a double in one of the largest companies on the stock market in a little over a year. In 2017, it trades at $165 and will pay out $2.28 per share in dividends.

Apple is a good example of the power of the Acquirer's Multiple, which identifies this type of stock, undervalued with a depressed value. It offers two ways to win. An activist emerges to improve the value and rapidly close the discount, or mean reversion acts on the price to push it up gradually in the meantime.

We wrote about Apple in April 2013 (four months before Icahn started tweeting about it):[65]

Tobias Carlisle ✔
@Greenbackd

AAPL offers exceptional franchise characteristics + is among the cheapest of the cheap lg cap stocks on the market:

Does Apple, Inc. (NASDAQ:AAPL) Show Statistical Evidence...
We wrote an article for the April issue of Value Investing Letter giving an overview of Quantitative Value, discussing the quantitative value model outlined in the book, and applying it ...
greenbackd.com

LIKES
4

5:07 PM - 24 Apr 2013

Apple again traded into the top thirty cheapest stocks in our screener at around $90 in late April 2016. We wrote about it a second time then. Here's the tweet:[66]

Tobias Carlisle ✔
@Greenbackd

Last time $AAPL got this cheap (April 2013) we wrote about it here:

Does Apple, Inc. (NASDAQ:AAPL) Show Statistical Evidence...
We wrote an article for the April issue of Value Investing Letter giving an overview of Quantitative Value, discussing the quantitative value model outlined in the book, and applying it ...
greenbackd.com

RETWEETS   LIKE
6   1

7:19 AM - 27 Apr 2016

Eighteen months later, it was up more than 80 percent to $165.

11. THE ART OF DEEP-VALUE INVESTING

"I am sometimes attacked for imposing 'rules.' Nothing could be further from the truth. I hate rules. All I do is report on how [people] react to different stimuli....A hint perhaps but scarcely a rule."

—David Ogilvy, *Ogilvy on Advertising* (1983)

If you want the market return, buy the market. If you want to beat the market, you must do something different. That means buying only undervalued stocks, or *concentrating*.

The trade-off for concentration is twofold:

1. Concentrated portfolios tend to be more volatile than the broader stock market. This means they move around more, both up and down. Good days for the market can be great days for the portfolio. Bad days for the market can be terrible days for the portfolio.

2. Concentrated portfolios don't track the market. This is known as *tracking error*. It means concentrated portfolios can go down when the

market goes up and up when the market goes down. The second kind of tracking error—portfolio up, market down—is the good kind. But you won't notice.

In practice, you'll only notice when your concentrated portfolio is down while the market is up. Academics have found high tracking error is associated with good long-term performance. But the market can beat portfolios of undervalued stocks for a long time. Tracking error won't feel good then. No one said it would be easy.

Zigging is hard. Our guts scream at us to zag with the crowd. We know we should zig. But undervalued stocks are hard to buy. They own bad businesses. The growth has slowed, and the profits are falling; they're losing money, or they're headed to liquidation. That's why they're undervalued.

Graham knew it. He wrote in *Security Analysis*:[67]

If the profits had been increasing steadily it is obvious that the shares would not sell at so low a price. The objection to buying these issues lies in the probability, or at least the possibility, that earnings will decline or losses continue, and that the resources will be dissipated and the intrinsic value ultimately become less than the price paid.

We worry the stock price will keep dropping and the growth will keep slowing, the profits will keep falling, and the business will keep losing money. We expect the trend to continue. That's a mistake, but an easy one to make. The wrong decision—zagging with the crowd—feels right, while the correct decision—zigging—feels wrong. Following the trend is instinctive. Mean reversion is not. But the data show mean reversion is more likely. This has several consequences for investors.

1. Value is more important than the trend in earnings. Undervalued low- or no-growth stocks beat expensive high-growth stocks and by a wide margin. Mean reversion pushes up undervalued stocks and pushes down expensive ones.

2. Undervalued low- or no-growth stocks beat undervalued high-growth stocks. We expect undervalued high-growth stocks to beat undervalued low-growth stocks. We assume high-growth value stocks are good stocks at bargain prices. But the data show mean reversion acts on growth, too. It pushes down high-growth stocks and up low- or no-growth stocks.

3. Undervalued low-profit stocks beat undervalued high-profit stocks. Mean reversion pushes down on high profits and up on low or no profits.

Highly profitable stocks only beat the market if Buffett's moat protects the profits. Without the moat, highly profitable stocks will get beaten up by the competition. Mean reversion acts on profits to drag down winners and push up losers. Investors should use some common sense and natural skepticism about profit charts that march all the way to heaven.

It is a rare business that can resist competition. And such businesses are hard to identify. Buffett's great skill has been to find those with defensible moats, which are his wonderful businesses. For those of us without Buffett's talent, the more undervalued the stock, the better. This is contrarian investing. This is value investing.

The Broken-Leg Problem

"Most decisions should probably be made with somewhere around 70 percent of the information you wish you had. If you wait for 90 percent, in most cases, you're probably being slow. Plus, either way, you need to be good at quickly recognizing and correcting bad decisions. If you're good at course correcting, being wrong may be less costly than you think, whereas being slow is going to be expensive for sure."

—Jeff Bezos, "Shareholder Letter" (2017)

How do we look past the falling stock prices, the losses, and the crisis? We know undervalued stocks beat the market. But we get stuck on the bad headlines. We want to follow the crowd far away from these stocks. Our gut fails us here.

The issue is we struggle with uncertainty. Problems requiring us to guess at odds and choose between unknown future outcomes are a mystery. We prefer trends. This is true for even the best investors and cognitive behavior experts. If knowing that we make these mistakes isn't enough to stop making them, how *do* we stop?

Since the 1950s, social scientists have been testing the forecasts of experts against simple rules. Study after study has found simple rules beat the experts. Paul Meehl, a founding father in the field, said in 1986:[68]

> There is no controversy in social science which shows such a large body of qualitatively diverse studies

coming out so uniformly in the same direction as this one…predicting everything from the outcomes of football games to the diagnosis of liver disease and when you can hardly come up with a half a dozen studies showing even a weak tendency in favour of the clinician, it is time to draw a practical conclusion.

Meehl means this: for lots of problems, simple rules make better forecasts than experts. This is the *Golden Rule of Predictive Modeling*.[69]

Value investors follow a simple rule like this:

- Buy if the price is much less than the value. Otherwise pass.

- Sell if the price is more than the value. Hold otherwise.

As long as value is always worked out the same way, for example, using the Acquirer's Multiple, Magic Formula, or some other method, this is a simple rule for value investing.

Many investors hate strict rules. They think it's better to use the output from the simple rule and then decide whether to follow it. This isn't a bad way to go. Experts make better decisions when they use simple rules. But they don't do as well as the simple rule alone.

This is the *broken-leg* problem. Suppose we have a rule for predicting whether John and Jane go to the movies together. If we know John has a broken leg, can we ignore the simple rule and make our own decision?

The argument is the simple rule will get the question wrong because it doesn't know John's leg is broken. Surely, we can include this data to decide that John and Jane will stay home. Won't that make our prediction more accurate? The studies find that it does not. The reason is we find more broken legs than there are. We make our own decisions too often, including too much irrelevant data.

This is true for companies with bad businesses, slowing growth, falling profits, or losses. As a portfolio, fair businesses at wonderful prices beat the market. But these companies look like they have broken legs. They have lots of reasons to override the simple rule and make their own decisions. We are better off if we just follow the simple rule.

Do It Yourself

"Marine Salvage—A science of vague assumptions based on debatable figures taken from inconclusive experiments and performed with instruments of problematic accuracy by persons of doubtful reliability and questionable mentality"

—C. A. Bartholomew, *Mud, Muscle, and Miracles: Marine Salvage in the United States Navy*, Department of Navy, 2010.

One simple rule for beating the market is to buy a portfolio of undervalued stocks. The acquirersmulitple.com website is a good source of ideas. The most undervalued names in the biggest one thousand stocks are available in the Large Cap Screener for free forever. There are two other paid screeners covering every stock listed in the United States: the All Investable Screener, which is the biggest half of all stocks, and the Small and Micro Cap Screener, the smallest half of all stocks.

The larger companies found in the Large Cap Screener have historically generated lower volatility and lower returns. Volatility is a fancy name for stocks going up and down. Higher volatility means the portfolio goes up and down more. Lower volatility means the portfolio goes up and down less.

The smaller companies found in the Small and Micro Cap Screener have historically generated higher absolute returns but had much greater portfolio volatility. The broadest screener, the All Investable Screener, gives the best balance of return and volatility.

How to Use the Screeners

There are two basic approaches to using the screeners that we call *business owner* and *quant investor*.

The *quant investor* uses the screeners to create a portfolio. He or she relies on the performance of the portfolio as a whole. The quant investor buys stocks from the screener without fear or favor and ignores the particular problems facing any given stock. And the investor ruthlessly plays the odds, taking a long-term portfolio approach to beating the market.

The *business owner* uses the screeners as a launching pad for further research. He or she studies each stock the way a classic, fundamental investor would: as a business. The business owner buys a stock in the screener only if it trades at a big-enough discount to value to provide a margin of safety, and he or she passes otherwise.

Both are equally valid approaches, but the business owner is by far and away the more difficult of the two. Most investors will be better off as quantitative investors. Consider this: most professional investors can't beat the market. (And when we say most, we mean 80 percent of professional investors.)

The reasons most people lag the market: cognitive biases and behavioral errors.

Joel Greenblatt has found that investors struggle to implement his Magic Formula in practice. In a great piece published in 2012, "Adding Your Two Cents May Cost You A Lot Over The Long Term," Greenblatt examined the first two years of returns to his firm's US separately managed accounts.

He gave his clients two choices to invest in US stocks. One account was like the business owner. The other was like the quant investor.

The business-owner account picked what top-ranked stocks to buy or sell and when to make these trades. The quant investor account followed a systematic process that bought and sold top-ranked stocks automatically.

Greenblatt conducted a great real-time behavioral investing experiment. Business-owner accounts had discretion over buy and sell decisions, while quant-investor accounts were automated. Both chose from the same list of stocks. So, what happened?

The business-owner accounts didn't do badly. Those accounts averaged 59.4 percent after all expenses over the two years, a good return. But the S&P 500 rose 62.7 percent over the same two years.

The quant-investor accounts averaged 84.1 percent after all expenses over the same two years, beating the business-owners by almost 25 percent (and the S&P 500 by well over 20 percent). That's a huge difference, particularly since both accounts chose stocks from the same list and were supposed to follow the same plan.

Greenblatt says, "The people who 'self-managed' their accounts took a winning system and used their judgment to unintentionally eliminate all the outperformance and then some!"

They took a simple rule that beat the market and used their own discretion to get beaten. Extraordinary! Greenblatt found the best-performing business-owner account didn't do anything. After the client opened the account, they bought stocks from the list and didn't touch them for the entire two years. The strategy of doing nothing beat the other business-owner accounts.

Greenblatt concluded, "I don't know if that's good news, but I like the message it appears to send—simply, when it comes to long-term investing, doing 'less' is often 'more.' Well, good work if you can get it, anyway."

The quant investor is by far and away the more boring of the two. Economist John Maynard Keynes wrote, "investment is intolerably boring and overexacting to anyone who is entirely exempt from the gambling instinct; whilst he who has it must pay to this propensity the appropriate toll." In other words, investing is boring if you don't like gambling. But if you like gambling, you pay a price.

Rules for Quant Investors

Use the screeners to select the top-ranked stocks from the Acquirer's Multiple database. Each screener finds the thirty best stocks at any time. You don't need to hold thirty positions. But you shouldn't hold fewer than twenty.

In general, holding more stocks leads to better diversification, which measures how many stocks you buy and how much money you put in each.

More stocks means less money in each stock. If a stock goes to zero, you'll lose less. If a stock goes up a lot, you'll make less. It's harder to manage because it means more buying and selling.

Fewer stocks means more money in each stock. If a stock goes to zero, you'll lose more. If a stock goes up a lot, you'll make more. Fewer stocks means less buying and selling. This is a simple method for investing systematically:

1. **Research:** Ignore any stocks you do not want to own for any reason. Hold at least twenty stocks for diversification.
2. **Buy:** It's best to buy all your stocks at once. But it's fine to *scale in*—make regular portfolio purchases over twelve months. One way to do it is to buy two or three stocks each month.
3. **Sell:** For taxable accounts, hold winners for one year plus one day. Then sell. That maximizes after-tax returns. If a stock is up and still in the screener after one year and one day, hold until it leaves the screener. If a stock is down and in the screener, hold. If a stock is down and leaves the screener, sell. You should check your stocks at least quarterly to see if you need to buy or sell.
4. **Rebalance:** Once you sell a stock, buy the next best stock in the screener you don't already hold.

The website acquirersmultiple.com has a screener for deep-value stocks listed in the United States and Canada. Sign up with the coupon "ZIG" to trial all screens for a month for 9.99 (80 percent off the regular price).

If you're intent on cherry-picking the best ideas in the screen, I've summarized the eight rules of deep value in the next chapter.

12. THE EIGHT RULES OF DEEP VALUE

"Survival is an infinite capacity for suspicion."
—John Le Carré, *Tinker, Tailor, Soldier, Spy* (1974)

"Very brave thing, in spying, to put your faith in someone. Any fool can go back to his desk and say, 'I don't altogether trust this chap. On the one hand, on the other hand.' It takes a lot of guts to take a flyer and say, 'I believe in him.'"
—John Le Carré, *The Pigeon Tunnel: Stories from My Life* (2016)

1. Zig when the crowd zags.

For any investment, we compare the crowd's view—the consensus—with our own. How do we find the consensus? It's revealed in the difference between the price of a stock and its value. We do our own research to work out the value. We look for stocks where our estimate diverges from the crowd's. In other words, we try to zig when the crowd zags.

Here's why: the only way to get a good price is to buy

what the crowd wants to sell and sell what the crowd wants to buy.

A *good* price implies a lopsided bet: a small downside and a big upside. The downside is small because the price already assumes the worst-case scenario. This creates a margin for error. If we're wrong, we won't lose much. If we're right, we'll make a lot. An upside bigger than the downside means we breakeven, even if we err more often than we succeed. If we manage to succeed as often as, or more often than we err, we'll do well.

Undervalued and out-of-favor companies offer lots of chances to zig—make contrarian bets. When a company owns a scary, bad, or boring business, the crowd overreacts or grows impatient and sells. That's how the stock becomes undervalued. Given time, many businesses turn out to be less scary, bad, or boring than they seem at first. The reason is mean reversion.

2. Buy undervalued companies.

The bigger the discount to value the better the return. This is true in the United States, United Kingdom, Europe, Africa, Asia, Australia, and New Zealand. It's true in developing and emerging markets. It's true globally. Deep discounts and good returns go together.

For most industrial companies, the Acquirer's Multiple is the best single measure of undervaluation. The Acquirer's Multiple is a company's enterprise value compared to its operating earnings. It is the metric private-equity firms use when buying companies whole and activist investors use when seeking hidden value.

The enterprise value is the *true* price we must pay for a company. It includes the market cap, which is the share price multiplied by the number of shares on issue. The market cap alone can mislead because it ignores other costs borne by the owner. The enterprise value also examines the balance-sheet and off-balance-sheet items. It rewards companies for cash, and it penalizes companies for debt, preferred stock, minority interests, and off-balance-sheet debts. These are all real costs paid by the owner.

Operating earnings is a measure of the income flowing from a business's operations. It excludes one-off items like sales of assets and legal settlements. We adjust operating earnings for interest and tax payments because it is affected by the capital structure: the mix of debt or equity. The adjustment makes possible an apples-to-apples comparison between two companies with different mixes of debt and equity.

For nonindustrial businesses like financials, such as banks and insurers, book value is the better single measure. Whatever the proxy, the goal is deep undervaluation.

3. Seek a margin of safety.

This is a threefold test of the discount to the valuation, the balance sheet, and the business.

First, the greater the company's discount to its value, the safer the purchase. A wide discount allows for errors and any decay in value. This is the corollary to the last rule that the biggest returns flow from the biggest discounts. It breaks the received wisdom of the market and academia that higher returns mean more risk. Here, the greater the margin of safety, the higher the returns and the lower the risk.

Second, on the balance sheet, we favor cash and other liquid securities over debt. We watch for off-balance sheet debts like leases and underfunded pensions. We look for credit issues and signs of financial distress. No company ever *won* with too much cash, but many have sunk with too much debt.

Finally, the company should own a *real* business. The business should have strong operating earnings with matching cash flow. Matching cash flows ensures the accounting earnings are real and not merely the figment of a clever embezzler's mind. We look for signs of earnings manipulation. Companies that own science experiments or toys in search of a business model are for speculators. But weak current profits in a stock with a good past record offers a good chance for mean reversion in those profits.

4. Treat a share as an ownership interest, not a mere ticker symbol.

A share is an ownership interest in a company. This has two implications:

First, a shareholder has rights as an owner of a company. Shareholders exercise those rights by voting at meetings.

Second, shareholders should pay attention to everything a company owns. That includes its business and its assets, chiefly its cash.

We look at both the business and the balance sheet to find financial robustness. A business can be worth a great deal, worthless, or worth less than nothing (if it's a regular money loser).

In the same way, a balance sheet can hold great value or have a negative net worth if the debt outweighs the assets.

Many investors follow profits—the fruits of the business—but ignore assets on the balance sheet. They ignore cash. A seemingly poor business with a strong balance sheet could represent hidden value. The asset value offers a free call option on any recovery in the business.

5. Be wary of high earnings growth and profits.

Mean reversion is a powerful force. It pushes down on fast growth rates and high profits, and it pushes up on low growth and losses.

Fast growth and good profits attract competition, which eats away at the growth and profit. Investors following Warren Buffett's example seek highly profitable businesses with a *moat*—a competitive advantage. But moats are harder to find and easier to cross than most investors realize.

Research shows most highly profitable companies' profits mean revert down over time. A small subset of businesses do earn persistent, high profits. But we have not yet been able to identify the causal factors *ex ante*—before the fact. In other words, we don't know beyond broad observations what factors predict steady growth and profits.

The evidence shows the odds of finding the next high-growth or high-profit stock are about the same as flipping a coin. Buffett's genius has been to identify these businesses. Mere mortals are better served buying at a steep discount to value.

The best place to find future growth and profit is in businesses currently enduring hard times. These businesses are also likely to trade at a wide discount to value. Buyers of these businesses can enjoy both an improvement in the business and a narrowing of the market-price discount.

6. Use simple, concrete rules to avoid making errors.

Cognitive errors happen when we make odds-based decisions about uncertain future outcomes. Investing in the stock market presents exactly this type of problem.

The secret to avoiding these errors is to use a set of simple, concrete rules. Ideally, we should write them down and strictly follow them.

Simple, concrete rules are testable. They should be back tested and battle tested. The back test makes sure the rules work over historical data sets, ideally in different countries and stock markets. The battle test makes sure the rules work in practice. No strategy has ever failed in theory. Almost all have failed in reality.

7. Concentrate, but not too much.

If you want to match the market, buy the market. If you want to beat the market, you must do something different. That means buying only the best ideas, or *concentrating*.

The trade-off for concentration is twofold:

1. Concentrated portfolios tend to be more volatile than the broader stock market. This means they move around more, both up and down. Good years for the market can be great years for the portfolio. Bad years for the market can be terrible years for the portfolio.

2. Concentrated portfolios don't closely follow the market. We call this "tracking error." It means concentrated portfolios can go down when the market goes up and up when the market goes

down. The second kind of tracking error—portfolio up, market down—is great to have. But you won't notice it. You'll only notice when your concentrated portfolio is down while the market is up. Academics have found high tracking error to be associated with good long-term performance. But the market can beat portfolios of undervalued stocks for a long time. Tracking error won't feel good then.

Don't become too concentrated. Assume your calculations and thinking are wrong. Remember, it's more likely you are wrong and the rest of the market is right.

8. Aim to maximize after-tax gains over the long term.

Our aim is to maximize the real, after-tax return over the long term. This has three important implications:

1. Thinking long term—beyond the next few quarters or years—offers a huge advantage to investors. Companies often become mispriced because the next year or so looks tough. This creates a good spot for investors willing to lag over the short term. We call this *time arbitrage*. It offers an enduring edge available to patient investors, no matter the size of their portfolio.

2. The effects of compounding take a long time to become observable. But interest on interest or gains on gains become significant over the long term.

3. Taxes and fees are hidden enemies of long-term compounding. High-fee mutual funds and other flow-through vehicles will struggle to beat

passive indexes. But low-fee, active exchange-traded funds are more tax efficient and can do so over the long term.

Value investing is a logical, time-tested investment method. The best value investors zig while others zag. They maximize their margin of safety and minimize their costs and taxes. They treat high growth and profits skeptically. And they assume their calculations and thinking are wrong. Skepticism, humility, and low costs maximize our chances of surviving. With luck and time, we can beat the market.

You can find stocks meeting these rules on the website acquirersmultiple.com—home of The Acquirer's Multiple stock screeners.

If you'd like to read more, please check out my other books:

- *Deep Value: Why Activists Investors and Other Contrarians Battle for Control of Losing Corporations* (2014, Wiley Finance)
- *Concentrated Investing: Strategies of the World's Greatest Concentrated Value Investors* (2016, Wiley Finance)
- *Quantitative Value: A Practitioner's Guide to Automating Intelligent Investment and Eliminating Behavioral Errors* (2012, Wiley Finance).

You can find me on Twitter @greenbackd.

If you enjoyed this book, I'd love a review on Amazon or Goodreads. Good reviews help spread the word.

APPENDIX: SIMULATION DETAILS

"A scrutiny so minute as to bring an object under an
untrue angle of vision, is a poorer guide to a man's
judgment than a sweeping glance which sees things in their
true proportion."
—Alexander Kinglake, *The Invasion of the Crimea* (1863)

This appendix contains the details of the simulations.
You can live a long and fruitful life without reading this part.
But I know there are some who won't be satisfied without
it. So here it is.

Assumptions

1. The historical simulation results do not represent the
results of actual trading and may not reflect the impact that
material economic and market factors may have had on an
investor's decision if the investor was actually managing
money. The simulated results were achieved through the
retroactive application of a model designed with the benefit
of hindsight. No investment strategy or risk-management
technique can guarantee return or eliminate risk in any
market environment.

2. In the simulation, Standard & Poor's Compustat database was used as a source for all information about companies and securities for the entire simulated time period. From 1987 to 2017, Compustat's Snapshot (point-in-time) database was used such that the simulation processed financial data concurrent with the time that the financial data became available to the public. Prior to 1987, the period when the timing of company financial data releases has been less comprehensively cataloged, the simulations assume that financial data was not available to investors until ninety days following the end of the applicable fiscal quarter.

3. The simulations were restricted to nonfinancial companies listed on the NYSE, NASDAQ, and AMEX stock exchanges.

4. Companies in the investable universe were ranked by earnings yield and return on invested capital (ROIC). In each of the simulations, these ranks were combined by a specific weighting of earnings yield and ROIC.

5. To minimize the potential impact, positive or negative, of market timing and to show how an equally weighted thirty-position portfolio might have performed at each point in time, the portfolios were rebalanced monthly to equally weight the thirty securities in each portfolio.

6. The purchase- and sale-prices for a security were the volume-weighted average closing price for the security over the first ten trading days of each month. The simulations assumed a trading cost of $0.01 per share. The simulations also assumed a maximum participation of 10 percent of a target holding's daily volume over the ten-day trading window.

7. The simulation performance does not reflect the deduction of any investment advisory fees.

8. Simulated performance results have certain inherent limitations. No representation is being made that any model or model mix will achieve performance similar to that shown. Simulated performance and actual prior performance provide no guarantee of future performance.

$50 Million and Greater

Yearly Returns (1973 to 2017)

	S&P 500	Magic Formula	Acquirer's Multiple
1973	−16.8%	−48.6%	−37.0%
1974	−20.3%	−23.6%	−17.2%
1975	31.0%	73.6%	67.0%
1976	1.2%	64.2%	67.7%
1977	−12.5%	24.6%	28.3%
1978	12.0%	33.6%	32.0%
1979	14.2%	43.7%	43.2%
1980	13.5%	43.0%	49.0%
1981	−7.1%	5.1%	17.2%
1982	20.7%	35.3%	41.5%
1983	12.5%	48.0%	46.5%
1984	9.9%	−10.4%	5.7%
1985	17.9%	38.7%	46.7%
1986	29.4%	25.5%	34.7%
1987	−6.2%	−11.5%	−12.6%
1988	15.7%	40.8%	25.5%
1989	10.6%	21.2%	14.0%
1990	4.5%	−5.8%	−24.5%
1991	18.9%	73.9%	59.5%
1992	7.3%	16.8%	23.3%

1993	9.8%	1.1%	17.8%
1994	−2.3%	6.6%	−10.8%
1995	35.2%	20.5%	23.2%
1996	23.6%	32.7%	28.7%
1997	24.7%	13.5%	30.0%
1998	30.5%	1.8%	−5.8%
1999	9.0%	18.4%	22.9%
2000	−2.0%	23.9%	24.8%
2001	−17.3%	32.5%	57.3%
2002	−24.3%	26.1%	4.7%
2003	32.2%	65.4%	84.9%
2004	4.4%	31.5%	36.5%
2005	8.4%	8.0%	3.6%
2006	12.4%	11.6%	25.9%
2007	−4.2%	−1.8%	−11.7%
2008	−40.1%	−40.4%	−29.3%
2009	30.0%	51.6%	91.0%
2010	19.8%	15.8%	44.2%
2011	2.0%	−6.1%	−21.2%
2012	14.1%	3.8%	6.4%
2013	19.0%	50.9%	31.5%
2014	11.9%	6.9%	5.2%
2015	−2.7%	−19.5%	−13.2%
2016	17.5%	22.4%	29.5%
2017 Q1	4.6%	3.1%	−1.0%
Average	**7.1%**	**16.2%**	**18.5%**

$10,000 Invested in S&P 500, Pure Charlie, Magic Formula, and Acquirer's Multiple (1973 to 2017) Log

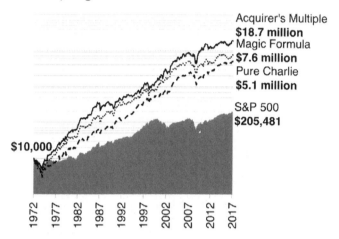

Acquirer's Multiple
$18.7 million
Magic Formula
$7.6 million
Pure Charlie
$5.1 million

S&P 500
$205,481

$10,000

$50 Million and Greater, Thirty Stocks

$50 Million Sample Statistics (1973 to 2017)

	Pure Charlie	Magic Formula	Acquirer's Multiple	S&P 500 TR
Return	15.1%	16.2%	18.6%	10.3%
Standard Dev.	19.4%	22.6%	23.2%	15.3%
Tracking Error	11.8%	15.0%	16.1%	N/A
Max Drawdown	69.5%	60.7%	51.2%	50.9%
Sharpe Ratio	0.53	0.50	0.59	0.36

Sortino Ratio	0.50	0.50	0.60	0.33
CAPM Alpha	4.3%	4.7%	7.0%	N/A
CAPM Beta	1.02	1.12	1.10	N/A
Correlation w S&P 500 TR	0.80	0.76	0.74	N/A

$200 Million and Greater

Yearly Returns (1973 to 2017)

	S&P 500	Magic Formula	Acquirer's Multiple
1973	−16.8%	−43.7%	−33.2%
1974	−20.3%	−22.6%	−22.2%
1975	31.0%	67.1%	59.2%
1976	1.2%	55.4%	60.5%
1977	−12.5%	20.4%	15.8%
1978	12.0%	32.2%	29.2%
1979	14.2%	47.9%	46.1%
1980	13.5%	42.5%	39.8%
1981	−7.1%	5.2%	4.4%
1982	20.7%	27.1%	28.3%
1983	12.5%	36.0%	40.2%
1984	9.9%	4.2%	15.3%
1985	17.9%	36.5%	33.2%
1986	29.4%	10.8%	22.9%
1987	−6.2%	−14.6%	−15.4%
1988	15.7%	50.2%	34.5%
1989	10.6%	20.0%	16.2%
1990	4.5%	−4.0%	−16.2%

1991	18.9%	64.9%	44.9%
1992	7.3%	32.3%	26.8%
1993	9.8%	−4.6%	13.0%
1994	−2.3%	9.6%	2.1%
1995	35.2%	28.1%	27.4%
1996	23.6%	27.0%	34.9%
1997	24.7%	31.4%	26.9%
1998	30.5%	21.0%	−4.6%
1999	9.0%	11.6%	18.5%
2000	−2.0%	34.9%	20.9%
2001	−17.3%	29.7%	44.1%
2002	−24.3%	20.1%	15.3%
2003	32.2%	60.4%	61.7%
2004	4.4%	32.6%	40.9%
2005	8.4%	7.2%	16.0%
2006	12.4%	12.8%	24.5%
2007	−4.2%	4.7%	−10.0%
2008	−40.1%	−37.3%	−32.1%
2009	30.0%	40.8%	66.2%
2010	19.8%	18.2%	39.4%
2011	2.0%	−2.7%	−11.5%
2012	14.1%	6.7%	14.3%
2013	19.0%	56.9%	42.1%
2014	11.9%	13.7%	1.4%
2015	−2.7%	−15.2%	−6.6%
2016	17.5%	11.8%	21.9%
2017 Q1	4.6%	2.2%	−2.8%
Average	**7.1%**	**17.2%**	**17.5%**

$10,000 Invested in S&P 500, Pure Charlie, Magic Formula, and Acquirer's Multiple (1973 to 2017) Log

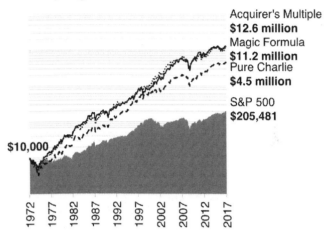

$200 Million and Greater, Thirty Stocks (1973 to 2017)

$200 Million Sample Statistics (1973 to 2017)

	Pure Charlie	Magic Formula	Acquirer's Multiple	S&P 500 TR
Return	14.8%	17.2%	17.5%	10.3%
Standard Dev.	19.3%	21.8%	22.4%	15.3%
Tracking Error	11.1%	13.6%	14.4%	N/A
Max Drawdown	66.9%	56.4%	54.5%	50.9%
Sharpe Ratio	0.52	0.57	0.57	0.36

Sortino Ratio	0.47	0.56	0.56	0.33
CAPM Alpha	3.9%	5.6%	5.8%	N/A
CAPM Beta	1.05	1.13	1.15	N/A
Correlation w S&P 500 TR	0.83	0.79	0.78	N/A

$1 Billion and Greater

Yearly Returns (1973 to 2017)

	S&P 500	Magic Formula	Acquirer's Multiple
1973	−16.8%	−33.9%	−31.2%
1974	−20.3%	−21.4%	−17.3%
1975	31.0%	53.6%	47.6%
1976	1.2%	52.0%	64.7%
1977	−12.5%	8.7%	11.3%
1978	12.0%	23.3%	19.9%
1979	14.2%	38.3%	47.1%
1980	13.5%	32.2%	29.6%
1981	−7.1%	0.2%	10.6%
1982	20.7%	21.3%	18.6%
1983	12.5%	26.9%	31.0%
1984	9.9%	9.4%	20.7%
1985	17.9%	40.3%	40.4%
1986	29.4%	20.4%	22.5%
1987	−6.2%	−3.1%	7.7%
1988	15.7%	28.0%	37.0%
1989	10.6%	17.2%	16.0%
1990	4.5%	6.0%	−7.9%
1991	18.9%	50.4%	36.9%

1992	7.3%	21.9%	25.3%
1993	9.8%	−0.6%	14.4%
1994	−2.3%	14.5%	15.1%
1995	35.2%	38.5%	36.6%
1996	23.6%	17.8%	18.1%
1997	24.7%	28.4%	28.4%
1998	30.5%	10.3%	−0.3%
1999	9.0%	8.5%	8.9%
2000	−2.0%	18.8%	16.1%
2001	−17.3%	39.1%	34.5%
2002	−24.3%	1.0%	−2.9%
2003	32.2%	51.6%	65.5%
2004	4.4%	25.5%	36.8%
2005	8.4%	19.4%	35.5%
2006	12.4%	19.7%	15.7%
2007	−4.2%	12.7%	8.2%
2008	−40.1%	−43.0%	−44.2%
2009	30.0%	56.7%	77.9%
2010	19.8%	7.5%	14.2%
2011	2.0%	13.0%	5.3%
2012	14.1%	5.6%	19.5%
2013	19.0%	54.2%	47.4%
2014	11.9%	17.4%	17.7%
2015	−2.7%	−8.8%	−11.6%
2016	17.5%	9.3%	15.3%
2017 Q1	4.6%	5.0%	1.0%
Average	**7.1%**	**16.2%**	**17.9%**

$10,000 Invested in S&P 500, Pure Charlie, Magic Formula, and Acquirer's Multiple (1973 to 2017) Log

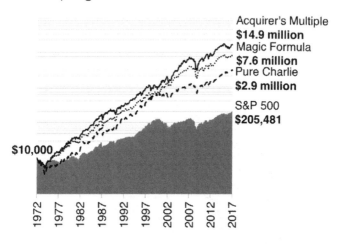

$1 Billion and Greater, Thirty Stocks

$1 Billion Sample Statistics (1973 to 2017)

	Pure Charlie	Magic Formula	Acquirer's Multiple	S&P 500 TR
Return	13.7%	16.2%	17.9%	10.3%
Standard Dev.	19.6%	20.3%	21.4%	15.3%
Tracking Error	10.0%	11.2%	12.8%	N/A
Max Drawdown	65.2%	54.2%	57.8%	50.9%
Sharpe Ratio	0.45	0.56	0.61	0.36

Sortino Ratio	0.43	0.54	0.61	0.33
CAPM Alpha	2.5%	4.7%	6.3%	N/A
CAPM Beta	1.12	1.13	1.13	N/A
Correlation w S&P 500 TR	0.87	0.85	0.81	N/A

Notes

[1] Warren Buffett, "The Superinvestors of Graham-and-Doddsville," *Columbia Business*, May 17, 1984.

[2] Shaun Tully, "The hottest investor in America," *Fortune*, May 30, 2007.

[3] Shaun Tully, "The hottest investor in America," *Fortune*, May 30, 2007.

[4] Shaun Tully, "The hottest investor in America," *Fortune*, May 30, 2007.

[5] Michael Steinhardt, "No Bull: My Life In and Out of Markets," *Wiley*, May 2, 2008.

[6] Ray Dalio, "The Culture Principle," *The New York Times Conferences*, March 7, 2017. Available at https://www.youtube.com/watch?v=h2KHec3KNyQ

[7] Howards Marks, "The Most Important Thing Illuminated: Uncommon Sense for the Thoughtful Investor, *Columbia Business School Publishing*, April 17, 2012

[8] Andy Rachleff, "Demystifying Venture Capital Economics, Part 1," *Wealthfront*. June 19, 2014. Available at https://blog.wealthfront.com/venture-capital-economics/

[9] Charlie Rose interview with Michael Steinhardt, *Charlie Rose Show, PBS*, December 21, 2001. Available at http://www.charlierose.com/view/interview/2766

[10] Seth Klarman, Speech to Columbia Business School on October 2, 2008, Reproduced in *Outstanding Investor Digest* 22, nos.1-2 (March 17, 2009): 3.

[11] Benjamin Graham, "Stock Market Study. Hearings Before The Committee on Banking and Currency, United States Senate, Eighty-Fourth Congress, First Session on Factors Affecting the

Buying and Selling of Equity Securities." (March 3, 1955*) United States Government Printing Office.* Washington. 1955. Available at http://www4.gsb.columbia.edu/filemgr?file_id=131668.

[12] Jeremy Grantham, Jeremy Grantham, Barron's (c. 2006), via Katsenelson, *The Little Book of Sideways Markets.*

[13] Warren Buffett, "Mr. Buffett on the Stock Market," *Fortune,* November 11, 1999. Available at http://archive.fortune.com/magazines/fortune/fortune_archive /1999/11/22/269071/index.htm.

[14] Seth Klarman, "Margin of Safety: Risk-Averse Value Investing Strategies for the Thoughtful Investor," *HarperColins,* October 1991.

[15] Warren Buffett. "Chairman's Letter." *Berkshire Hathaway, Inc. Annual Report,* 1989. Available at http://www.berkshirehathaway.com/letters/1989.html

[16] Warren Buffett, "Letter to Partners, 1961," *Buffett Partnership.* Available at https://www.pragcap.com/warren-buffett-partnership-letters/

[17] Warren Buffett, "Letter to Partners, 1961," *Buffett Partnership.* Available at https://www.pragcap.com/warren-buffett-partnership-letters/

[18] Warren Buffett, "Letter to Partners, 1961," *Buffett Partnership.* Available at https://www.pragcap.com/warren-buffett-partnership-letters/

[19] Warren Buffett, "Letter to Partners, 1961," *Buffett Partnership.* Available at https://www.pragcap.com/warren-buffett-partnership-letters/

[20] Alice Schroeder, "The Snowball: Warren Buffett and the Business of Life," *Bantam,* September 29, 2008.

[21] Warren Buffett. "Chairman's Letter." *Berkshire Hathaway, Inc. Annual Report,* 1985. Available at http://www.berkshirehathaway.com/letters/1985.html

[22] Janet Lowe, "Damn Right: Behind the Scenes with Berkshire Hathaway Billionaire Charlie Munger," *Wiley,* May 9, 2003.

[23] Janet Lowe, "Damn Right: Behind the Scenes with Berkshire Hathaway Billionaire Charlie Munger," *Wiley*, May 9, 2003.

[24] Janet Lowe, "Damn Right: Behind the Scenes with Berkshire Hathaway Billionaire Charlie Munger," *Wiley*, May 9, 2003.

[25] Alice Schroeder, "The Snowball: Warren Buffett and the Business of Life," *Bantam*, September 29, 2008.

[26] Alice Schroeder, "The Snowball: Warren Buffett and the Business of Life," *Bantam*, September 29, 2008.

[27] Alice Schroeder, "The Snowball: Warren Buffett and the Business of Life," *Bantam*, September 29, 2008.

[28] Alice Schroeder, "The Snowball: Warren Buffett and the Business of Life," *Bantam*, September 29, 2008.

[29] Alice Schroeder, "The Snowball: Warren Buffett and the Business of Life," *Bantam*, September 29, 2008.

[30] Alice Schroeder, "The Snowball: Warren Buffett and the Business of Life," *Bantam*, September 29, 2008.

[31] Warren Buffett. "Chairman's Letter." *Berkshire Hathaway, Inc. Annual Report,* 1989. Available at
http://www.berkshirehathaway.com/letters/1989.html

[32] Warren Buffett. "Chairman's Letter." *Berkshire Hathaway, Inc. Annual Report,* 2007. Available at
http://www.berkshirehathaway.com/letters/2007.html.

[33] Warren Buffett. "Chairman's Letter." *Berkshire Hathaway, Inc. Annual Report,* 1991. Available at
http://www.berkshirehathaway.com/letters/1991.html.

[34] Warren Buffett. "Chairman's Letter." *Berkshire Hathaway, Inc. Annual Report,* 1989. Available at
http://www.berkshirehathaway.com/letters/1989.html

[35] Warren Buffett. "Chairman's Letter." *Berkshire Hathaway, Inc. Annual Report,* 1988. Available at
http://www.berkshirehathaway.com/letters/1988.html

[36] Benjamin Graham and David Dodd. *Security Analysis: The Classic 1934 Edition.* McGraw Hill 1934.

[37] Warren Buffett. "Chairman's Letter." *Berkshire Hathaway, Inc. Annual Report,* 1989. Available at
http://www.berkshirehathaway.com/letters/1989.html

[38] Roger Lowenstein, "Buffett: The Making of an American Capitalist," *Random House.* July 24, 2013.

[39] Joel Greenblatt, "The Little Book That Beats the Market (Little Books. Big Profits)," *Wiley*, April 21, 2008.

[40] Joel Greenblatt, "The Little Book That Beats the Market (Little Books. Big Profits)," *Wiley*, April 21, 2008.

[41] Warren Buffett. "Chairman's Letter." *Berkshire Hathaway, Inc. Annual Report,* 2014. Available at http://www.berkshirehathaway.com/letters/2014.html

[42] Warren Buffett. "Chairman's Letter." *Berkshire Hathaway, Inc. Annual Report,* 1993. Available at http://www.berkshirehathaway.com/letters/1993.html

[43] James Montier. "The Little Note that Beats the Market." *DrKW Macro Research*, March 9, 2006.

[44] Tim Loughran and Jay W. Wellman. "New Evidence on the Relation Between the Enterprise Multiple and Average Stock Returns (September 5, 2010)." Available at SSRN: http://ssrn.com/abstract=1481279 or http://dx.doi.org/10.2139/ssrn.1481279.

[45] Benjamin Graham. "A Conversation with Benjamin Graham." Financial Analysts Journal, Vol. 32, No. 5 (1976), pp. 20–23.

[46] J. Greenblatt, R. Pzena, and B. Newberg. "How the small investor can beat the market." *The Journal of Portfolio Management*, Summer 1981, 48–52.

[47] Michelle Clayman. "In Search of Excellence: The Investor's Veiwpoint." *Financial Analysts Journal*, May–June 1987, 54. Suggested by Damodaran, 2012

[48] Barry B. Bannister and Jesse Cantor. "In Search of "Un-Excellence"—An Endorsement of Value-style Investing" *Stifel Financial Corp.* July 16, 2013.

[49] Mark Stevens, *King Icahn* (New York: Penguin Group, 1993).

[50] Mark Stevens, *King Icahn* (New York: Penguin Group, 1993).

[51] Mark Stevens, *King Icahn* (New York: Penguin Group, 1993).

[52] Mark Stevens, *King Icahn* (New York: Penguin Group, 1993).

[53] Robert L. Chapman, Letter to J. Michael Wilson dated March 30, 2000, Exhibit A to Schedule 13D, March 31, 2000. Available

at
https://www.sec.gov/Archives/edgar/data/1017766/00010135
9400000097/0001013594-00-000097.txt

[54] Robert L. Chapman, Letter to J. Michael Wilson dated March 30, 2000, Exhibit A to Schedule 13D. Available at
https://www.sec.gov/Archives/edgar/data/1017766/00010135
9400000097/0001013594-00-000097.txt

[55] Robert L. Chapman, Exhibit A to Schedule 13D, February 7, 2001. Available at
https://www.sec.gov/Archives/edgar/data/1017766/00010135
9401000043/0001013594-01-000043.txt

[56] Daniel Loeb, "Letter to Chief Executive Officer," September 8, 2000. Available at
https://www.sec.gov/Archives/edgar/data/1040273/00008991
4000000393/0000899140-00-000393-0003.txt

[57] Daniel Loeb, "Letter to Chief Executive Officer," September 8, 2000. Available at
https://www.sec.gov/Archives/edgar/data/1040273/00008991
4000000393/0000899140-00-000393-0003.txt

[58] Daniel Loeb, "Letter to Chief Executive Officer," September 8, 2000. Available at
https://www.sec.gov/Archives/edgar/data/1040273/00008991
4000000393/0000899140-00-000393-0003.txt

[59] David Einhorn. "iPrefs: Unlocking Value." Greenlight Capital, 2013. Available
at https://www.greenlightcapital.com/905284.pdf.

[60] David Einhorn. "iPrefs: Unlocking Value." Greenlight Capital, 2013. Available
at https://www.greenlightcapital.com/905284.pdf.

[61] Carl Icahn, Letter to Tim Cook. Available at
https://www.cnbc.com/2013/10/24/carl-icahns-letter-to-tim-cook.html

[62] Carl C Icahn, Tweet, 11:21 AM, August 14, 2013. Available at
https://twitter.com/Carl_C_Icahn/statuses/3673502069933998
08

[63] David Einhorn. "iPrefs: Unlocking Value." *Greenlight Capital, 2013*. Available
at https://www.greenlightcapital.com/905284.pdf.
[64] Carl C Icahn, Tweet, 11:12 AM, 11:13 AM, August 19, 2014. Available at
https://twitter.com/Carl_C_Icahn/status/501794143413493760,
https://twitter.com/Carl_C_Icahn/status/501794076942172160,
https://twitter.com/Carl_C_Icahn/status/501793872159449089
[65] Author, Tweet, 5:07 PM, April 24, 2013. Available at
https://twitter.com/Greenbackd/status/327212261716398081
[66] Author, Tweet, 7:19 AM, April 27, 2016. Available at
https://twitter.com/Greenbackd/status/725328530167463936
[67] Benjamin Graham and David Dodd. *Security Analysis: The Classic 1934 Edition*. (New York: McGraw Hill) 1934.
[68] Michael A. Bishop. and J. D. Trout. "50 years of successful predictive modeling should be enough: Lessons for philosophy of science." *Philosophy of Science* 69.S3 (2002): S197–S208.
[69] Michael A. Bishop. and J. D. Trout. "50 years of successful predictive modeling should be enough: Lessons for philosophy of science." *Philosophy of Science* 69.S3 (2002): S197–S208.

37459327R00087

Made in the USA
Columbia, SC
29 November 2018